D0004755

A *Golden Hands* PATTERN BOOK

SEWING CHILDREN'S CLOTHES

A Golden Hands PATTERN BOOK

SEWING CHILDREN'S CLOTHES

RANDOM HOUSE NEW YORK

Photography by:
Steve Bicknell No. 32
Jim Williams Nos. 10, 24, 25, 29, 30, 31

Beta Pictures Nos. 34, 35, 36, 37, 38, 39, 40, 41, 42, 43,
44, 45, 46, 47, 48, 49, 50, 51, 52, 53, 54, 55, 56, 57, 58,
59, 60
Simis Press Nos. 1, 2, 3, 4, 5, 6, 7, 8, 9, 11, 12, 13, 14,
15, 16, 17, 18, 19, 20, 21, 22, 23, 26, 27, 28, 33

Designs by:
Valerie Punchard Nos. 24, 25, 29
Anita Skjold Nos. 31, 32

© Marshall Cavendish Limited, 1973

All rights reserved under International and Pan-
American Copyright Conventions. Published in the
United States by Random House, Inc., New York,
and simultaneously in Canada by Random House of
Canada Limited, Toronto.
Originally published in Great Britain by Marshall
Cavendish Limited under the title *The Golden
Hands Book of 60 Things to Sew for Children.*

Library of Congress Cataloging in Publication Data
Main entry under title:
Sewing children's clothes.
1. Children's clothing—Pattern design.
I. Golden hands.
TT640.S48   646.4'06   73-5017
ISBN 0-394-48797-4

Manufactured in Great Britain
First American Edition

CONTENTS

1

*Playtime dungarees,
the straps cross at the
back and button
to the bib in front*

Fabric required

Sizes	1	3	yrs
36 inch fabric	$1\frac{1}{8}$	$1\frac{1}{4}$	yds
48 inch fabric	$\frac{7}{8}$	1	yd
$\frac{1}{2}$ inch wide			
Elastic	$\frac{3}{8}$	$\frac{3}{8}$	yd
Buttons	4	4	

To make pattern
See Know-how.

To cut out
See Know-how. Open out fabric and pin
piece No. 3 on single layer. *Remember to add
turnings and hem allowances.* $\frac{3}{4}$ inch casing for
elastic is allowed.

Making the dungarees
Stitch side leg seams, leaving $4\frac{1}{2}$ inches open
at top edges. Press. See Working Details,
making up pants. Hem edges of side
openings. At back waist, turn $1\frac{1}{4}$ inches to
wrong side. Press. This forms casing for
elastic. Turn in raw edge and topstitch. Cut
elastic to fit back waist comfortably, thread
through casing and secure ends. Fold tabs in
half, right sides together, stitch points and
side edges, turn right side out. Make a
horizontal buttonhole in tab (see Working
Details). Slip unstitched edges in ends of
elastic casing and stitch firmly in place. Fold
bib in half, right sides together, stitch side
seams. Turn right side out. Press. Stitch to
front waist, right sides together. Make neat
remainder of waist seam. Press. Fold
shoulder straps in half lengthwise, right sides
together, stitch pointed end and long edge.
Turn right side out. Make buttonhole in
pointed end. Stitch straps in place at back.
Sew buttons to waist and bib top edge to
correspond to buttonholes. Fold pockets
in half, right sides together, stitch side and
lower edges, leaving gap through which to
turn pockets right side out. Slip stitch
openings. Stitch pockets in place. Stitch
pants hems.
Remember—each square equals one inch square.

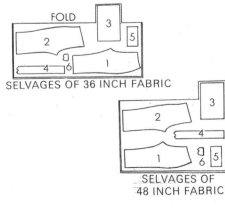

SELVAGES OF 36 INCH FABRIC

SELVAGES OF
48 INCH FABRIC

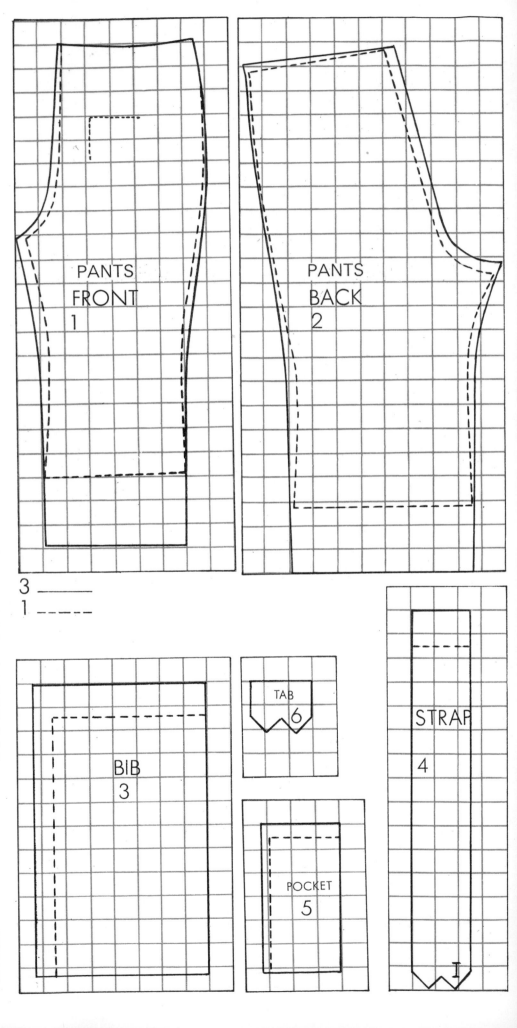

PANTS
FRONT
1

PANTS
BACK
2

3 ———
1 － － －

BIB
3

TAB
6

STRAP
4

POCKET
5

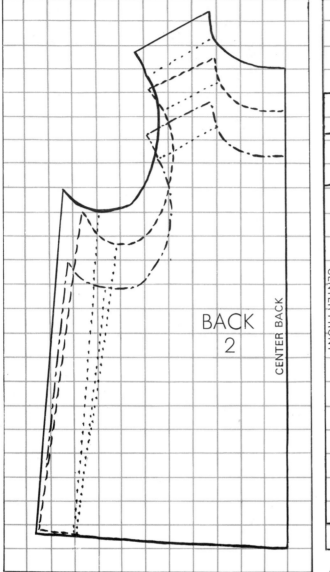

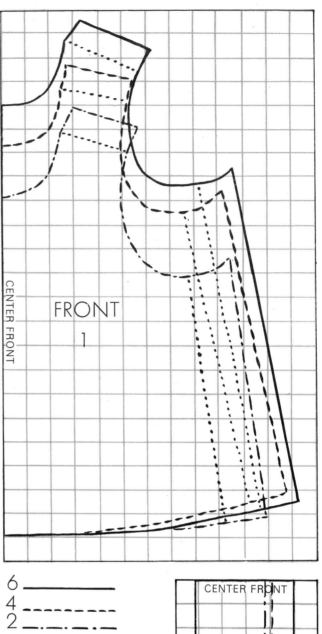

CENTER BACK

BACK
2

CENTER FRONT

FRONT
1

6 —————
4 – – – – –
2 –·—·—·—

BACK
FRILL
4

CENTER BACK

CENTER FRONT

FRONT
FRILL

3

2

*Pinafore dress
buttoned on each shoulder
and down one side, with a
deep frill around the hem*

Fabric required

Sizes	2	4	6	yrs
36 inch fabric	1⅜	1½	1¾	yds
48 inch fabric	¾	⅞	1	yd
Bias binding	1½	1½	1½	yds
Buttons	8	8	8	

To make pattern
See Know-how.

To cut out
See Know-how. *Please note:* ⅝ inch turning
is allowed for right-hand side seam. 1½ inch
facing for side opening. Add ¼ inch turning
at lower edge of pieces Nos. 1 and 2 and at
one short end and lower edge of pieces Nos.
3 and 4. No turnings are necessary on
bound edges. Fold 48 inch fabric with
selvages meeting at center and place pieces
Nos. 1 and 2 on folds as shown. Refold
remaining fabric lengthwise to place pieces
Nos. 3 and 4 on fold.

Making the pinafore dress
For right-hand side seam trim off 1½ inches
at right side edge of front and back. Stitch
seam, taking ⅝ inch turnings. Press. Fold in
1½ inches for facing on remaining side edges
and baste in place. Fold in 1 inch on all
shoulder edges and slip stitch in place. Bind
neck and armhole edges with bias binding
(see Working Details). Join the two frill
pieces into one length. Narrowly hem one
long edge and the two short ends. Gather
remaining edge to fit dress hem as far as
facings. Open out facings at lower edge.
With right sides together, raw edges even,
pin and baste frill to lower edge of dress,
matching seams. Stitch. Turn facings to
inside and slip stitch in place. Make two
vertical buttonholes (see Working Details)
in each front shoulder, ⅜ inch from fold, and
on front side opening make four vertical
buttonholes ⅝ inch from edge. Sew on
buttons to correspond to buttonholes.
Remember—each square equals one inch square.

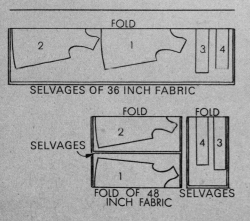

SELVAGES OF 36 INCH FABRIC

SELVAGES · FOLD · FOLD · SELVAGES · FOLD OF 48 INCH FABRIC

3 | **4**

Sunny toweling top with a big patch pocket and matching pants | *Cover-up beach coat with a hood and zippered front*

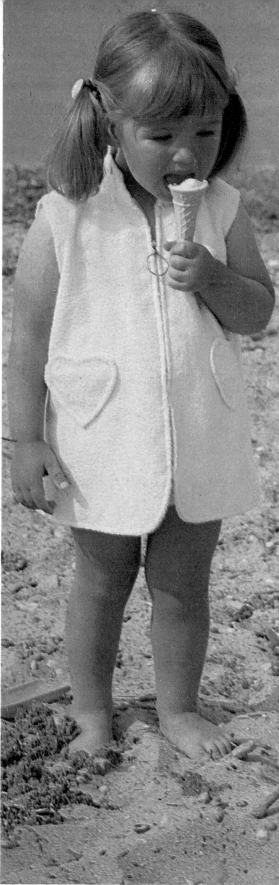

5 | 6

Back-buttoned sun top and matching pants for the beach

Adorable sleeveless beach robe with heart shaped pockets

3

Sunny toweling top

Fabric required

Sizes	2	4	6	yrs
36 inch fabric	$1\frac{3}{8}$	$1\frac{1}{2}$	$1\frac{5}{8}$	yds
48 inch fabric	$1\frac{1}{8}$	$1\frac{1}{4}$	$1\frac{3}{8}$	yds
Bias binding	2	2	2	yds
$\frac{1}{4}$ inch wide elastic	$\frac{3}{4}$	$\frac{3}{4}$	$\frac{3}{4}$	yd
Button	1	1	1	

To make pattern

See Know-how.

To cut out

See Know-how. Fold 48 inch fabric in from each side, then cut and fold as usual. *Remember to add turnings.* No turnings are necessary on bound edges.

Making the shirt and pants

Shirt

Stitch shoulder, side and sleeve seams. Stitch center back seam below neck opening. Stitch sleeves into armholes, (see Working Details). Bind neck edge (see Working Details). Hem sleeve edges. Stitch button and loop to fasten back neck. Make neck opening neat. Bind edges of pocket with bias binding, stitch in place. Hem lower edge.

Pants

See Working Details, making up panties. *Remember—each square equals one inch square.*

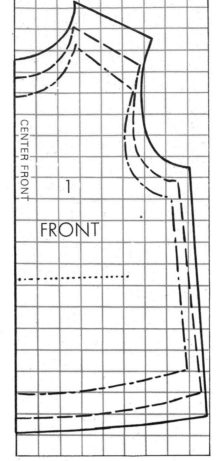

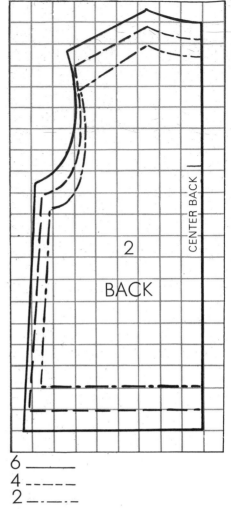

6 ——————
4 – – – – –
2 –·—·—·—

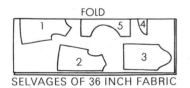

SELVAGES OF 36 INCH FABRIC

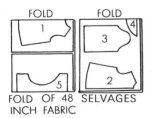

FOLD OF 48 SELVAGES
INCH FABRIC

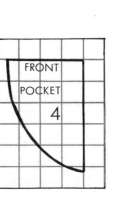

FRONT
POCKET
4

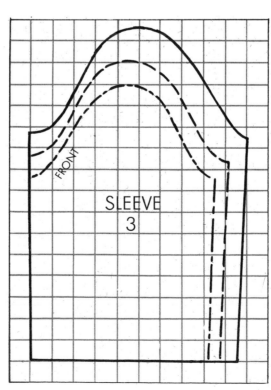

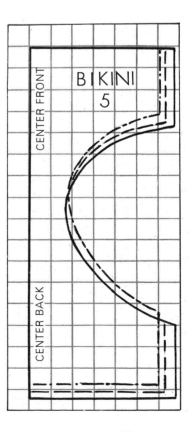

4

Beach coat with hood

Fabric required

Sizes	2	5	yrs
36 inch fabric	$1\frac{7}{8}$	$2\frac{1}{8}$	yds
48 inch fabric	$1\frac{7}{8}$	$1\frac{1}{4}$	yds
Zipper			
(open end)	16	20	in
Bias binding	2	2	yds

To make pattern
See Know-how.

To cut out
See Know-how. *Remember to add turnings and hem allowances.* No turnings are necessary on bound edges.

Making the beach coat
Stitch shoulder darts. Press. Stitch shoulder, side and sleeve seams. Press. Stitch sleeves into armholes (see Working Details). Stitch darts in each hood section. Stitch center seam in hood and topstitch each side of seam. Press. Bind front edge with bias binding (see Working Details). With right sides together, stitch hood to neck edge, bind raw edges. Insert zipper in front opening (see Working Details). With wrong sides together, baste pocket sections at outer edges. Bind edges. Stitch pockets in place. Hem sleeves and lower edge.
Remember—each square equals one inch square.

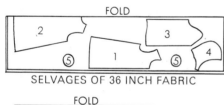

SELVAGES OF 36 INCH FABRIC

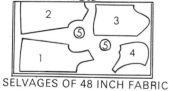

SELVAGES OF 48 INCH FABRIC

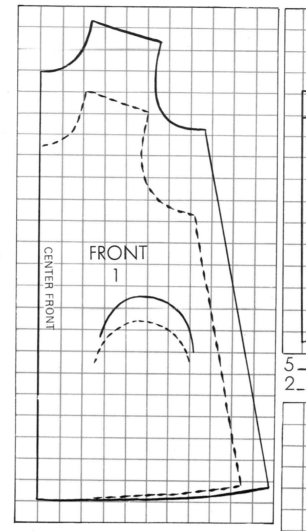

FRONT 1

CENTER FRONT

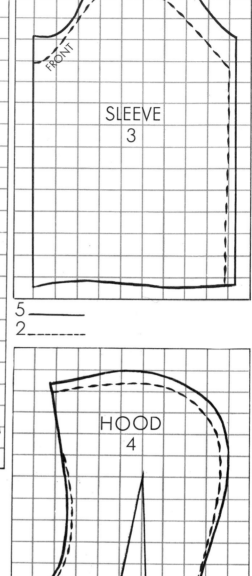

FRONT

SLEEVE 3

5 ——————
2 - - - - - - -

HOOD 4

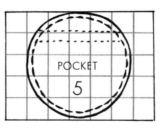

POCKET 5

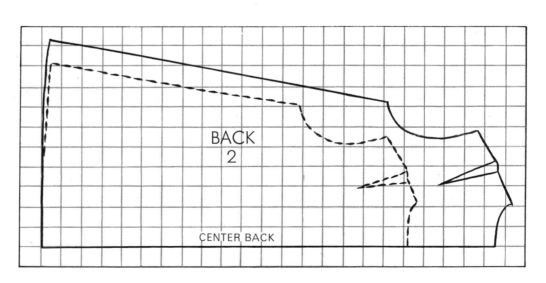

BACK 2

CENTER BACK

5 *Sun top and pants*

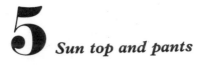

Fabric required

Sizes	2	4	6	yrs
36 inch fabric	$\frac{3}{4}$	$\frac{3}{4}$	$\frac{7}{8}$	yd
48 inch fabric	$\frac{1}{2}$	$\frac{1}{2}$	$\frac{5}{8}$	yd
Bias binding	3	3	3	yds
$\frac{1}{4}$ inch wide elastic	$1\frac{3}{4}$	$1\frac{3}{4}$	$1\frac{3}{4}$	yds
Buttons	2	2	2	

To make pattern
See Know-how.

To cut out
See Know-how. *Remember to add turnings.* No turnings are necessary on bound edges.

Making top and pants
Bikini top
Stitch shoulder and side seams. Press. Fold back facings onto wrong side at first dotted line from back edge. Bind neck, armholes and lower edge with bias binding (see Working Details). Make two buttonholes in right back, (see Working Details), sew buttons to correspond.

Bikini pants
See Working Details, making up panties. *Remember—each square equals one inch square.*

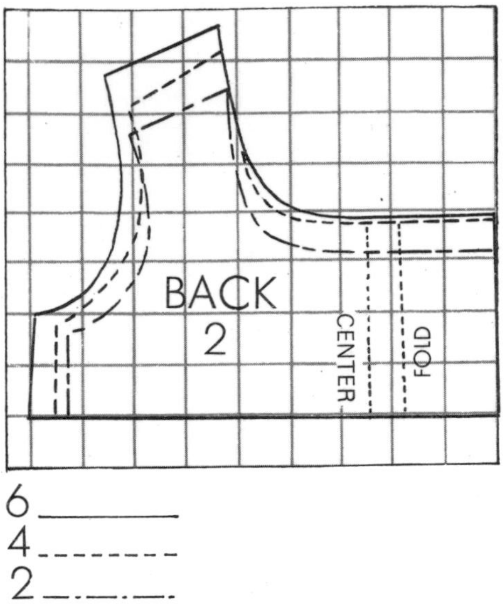
BACK
2
CENTER
FOLD
6
4
2

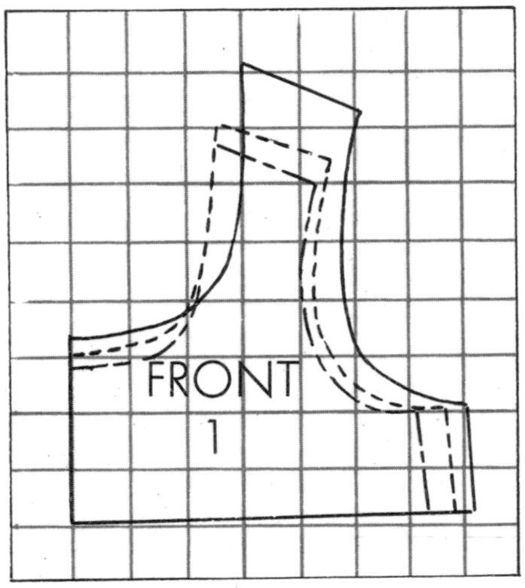
FRONT
1

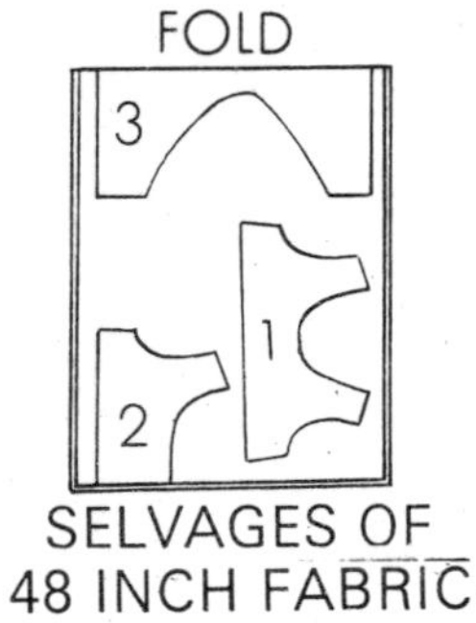
FOLD
3
1
2
SELVAGES OF
48 INCH FABRIC

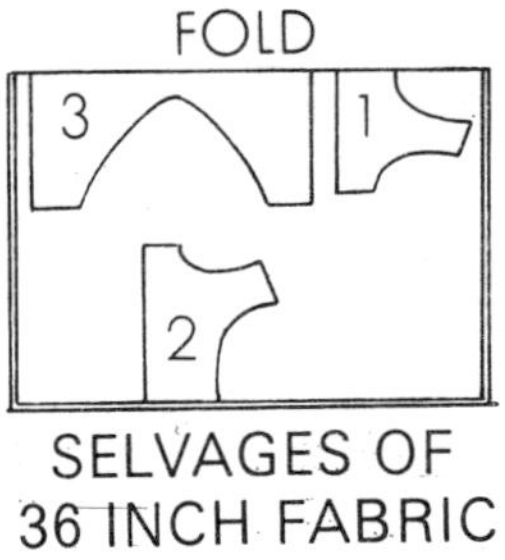
FOLD
3
1
2
SELVAGES OF
36 INCH FABRIC

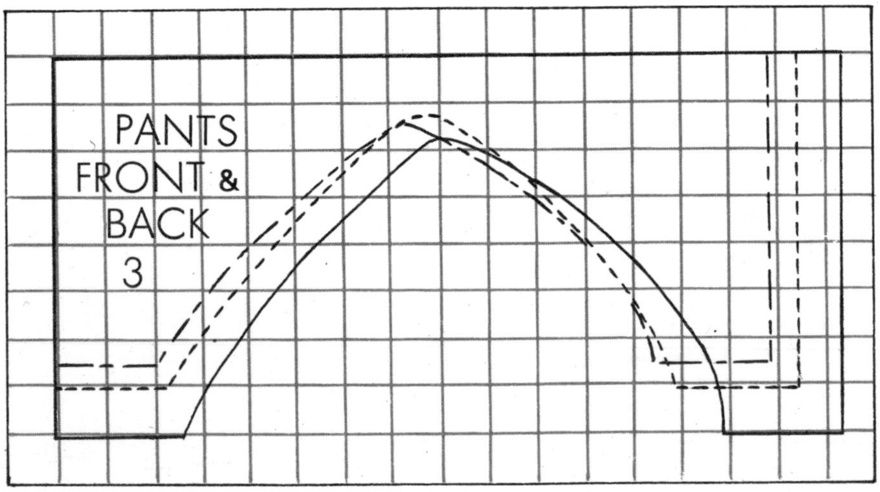
PANTS
FRONT &
BACK
3

6 *Sleeveless beach robe*

Fabric required

Sizes	5	7	9	yrs
36 inch fabric	$1\frac{3}{8}$	$1\frac{3}{4}$	2	yds
48 inch fabric	$1\frac{3}{8}$	$1\frac{1}{2}$	$1\frac{5}{8}$	yds
Zipper (open end)	15	18	20	in
$\frac{1}{4}$ inch wide elastic	$1\frac{3}{4}$	$1\frac{3}{4}$	$1\frac{3}{4}$	yds

To make pattern
See Know-how, also for patterns for armhole facings. Cut facing pattern for front hem, from beginning of curve to side seam, following line of curve.

To cut out
See Know-how. *Remember to add turnings.* Add normal hem allowance at back only, leaving $\frac{1}{2}$ inch turnings for facing front hems.

Making the beach robe
Dress
With right sides together, stitch facings to front hem sections. Snipping into curves, turn facings to inside. Stitch shoulder seams of dress, easing back on to front. Stitch facings to armholes, (see Working Details). With right sides together, opening facings and hem, stitch side seams. Turn up back hem and slip stitch front hem facing to dress. Make up and attach collar (see Working Details). Insert zipper in center front (see Working Details). With right sides together, stitch pocket sections in pairs, leaving small openings to turn through. Turn to right side and close opening. Stitch pockets in place.

Panties
See Working Details, making up panties. *Remember—each square equals one inch square.*

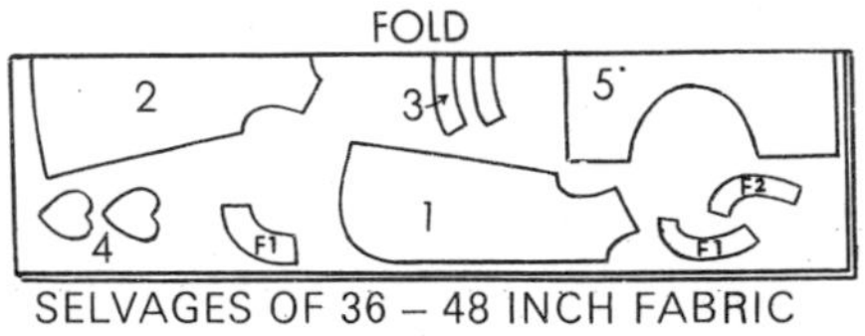
FOLD
2
3
5
1
4
F1
F2
F1
SELVAGES OF 36 – 48 INCH FABRIC

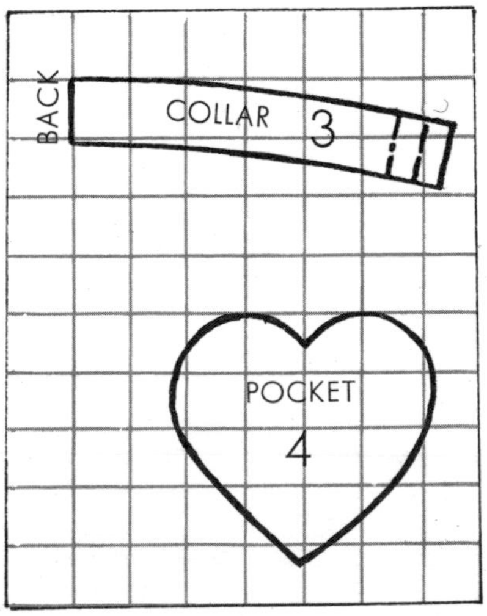
BACK
COLLAR
3
POCKET
4

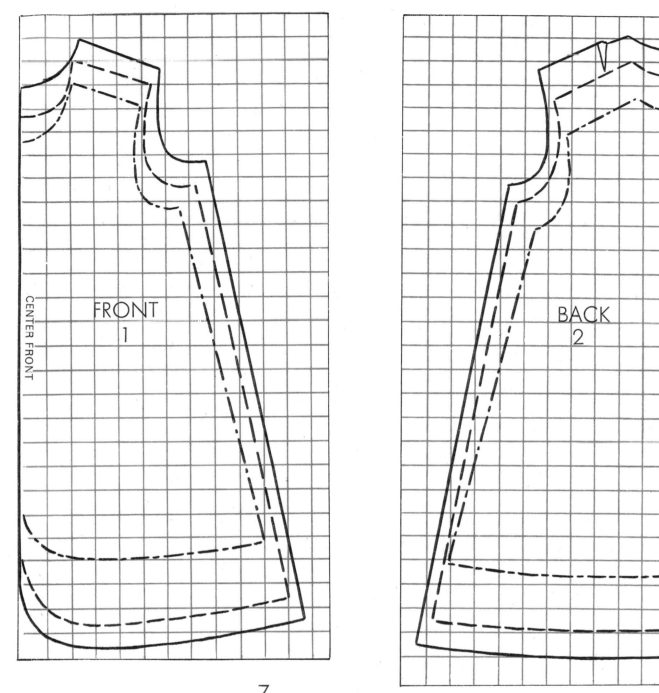

CENTER FRONT

FRONT
1

CENTER BACK

BACK
2

7 ——————
5 - - - - - - -
3 —·—·—·—

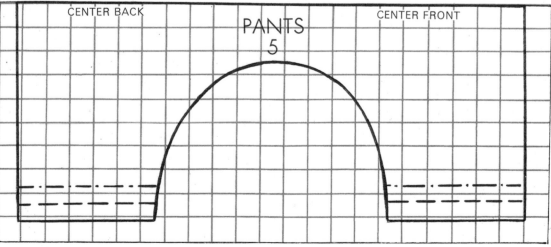

CENTER BACK   CENTER FRONT

PANTS
5

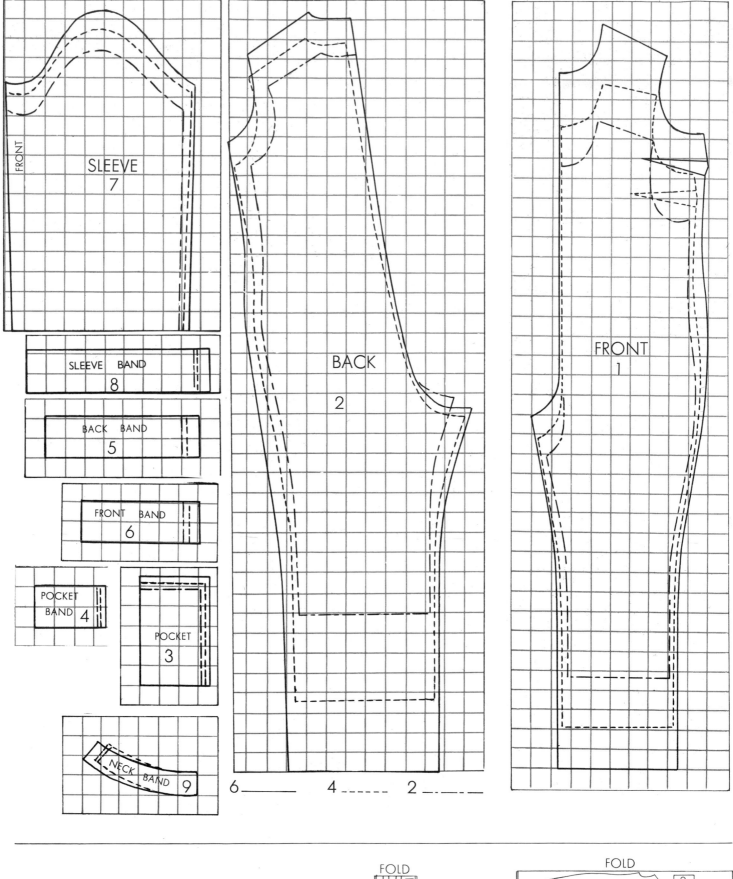

SLEEVE
7

FRONT

SLEEVE BAND
8

BACK BAND
5

FRONT BAND
6

POCKET BAND 4

POCKET
3

NECK BAND 9

BACK
2

FRONT
1

6_____ 4 ------ 2 —-—-

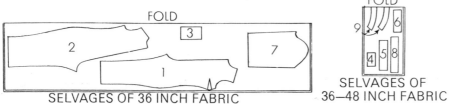

FOLD

2

3

7

1

SELVAGES OF 36 INCH FABRIC

FOLD

9

6

4 5 8

SELVAGES OF
36—48 INCH FABRIC

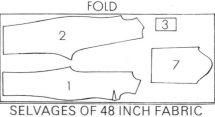

FOLD

2

3

7

1

SELVAGES OF 48 INCH FABRIC

16

7

All-in-one jumpsuit with a zip front, patch pockets and long sleeves

Fabric required

Sizes	2	4	6	yrs
36 inch fabric	1⅞	2⅛	2¼	yds
48 inch fabric	1⅜	1½	1¾	yds
Contrasting fabric	¼	¼	¼	yds
Zipper	12	12	14	in

To make pattern
See Know-how

To cut out
See Know-how. *Remember to add turnings.*

Making the jumpsuit
Make front darts. Stitch side seams. Stitch side seams in leg bands. Press. With right sides together, stitch one edge of band to leg edge. Fold leg bands in half onto wrong side, slip stitch in place. Stitch inner leg seams. Stitch two halves of garment together from center front below zipper opening to center back neck. Stitch shoulder seams. Press. Insert zipper into front opening (see Working Details). Stitch sleeve seams, first attaching sleeve bands as for legs. Stitch sleeves into armholes (see Working Details). Make up and attach collar (see Working Details). Stitch pocket bands to pockets, then fold pockets in half, right sides together and stitch pocket seams. Turn right side out. Press. Slip stitch bands in place and sew pockets to garment.
Remember—each square equals one inch square.

8

Crisp pants suit; the double-breasted long vest has a vent at the back

Fabric required

Sizes	3	5	yrs
48 inch fabric	1⅝	1¾	yds
54 inch fabric	1⅛	1½	yds
Zipper	6	6	ins
Buttons	8	8	
Snap fasteners	4	4	

To make pattern

See Know-how, also for patterns for neck and armhole facings. Front neck facing to join fold-back front bodice facing.

To cut out

See Know-how. *Remember to add turnings and hem allowances.* Cut waistband 2 inches wide, 26 inches long for Size 3 years and 27 inches long for Size 5 years.

Making pants suit

Long vest

Baste pleat at center back of skirt. Press. Stitch shoulder, side and center back seams of bodice, side seams of skirt. Press. Stitch neck and sleeve facings (see Working Details). Make two bound buttonholes on bodice (see Working Details) one on skirt, 2 inches apart for Size 3 years, 2½ inches apart for Size 5 years, measuring from what will be finished waist seam, make outer ends of buttonholes ⅝ inch from fold edge of vest. Join bodice to skirt, leaving a buttonhole space in the stitching even with other buttonholes. Press. Slip stitch facing to neck edge where it folds back. Topstitch ⅜ inch each side of waistline, also neck and armhole edges. Fold pockets in half, right sides together, stitch, leaving small space to turn pocket through to right side. Close opening, press and topstitch to vest. Sew on buttons. Turn up vest hem and slip stitch into place. Secure left side of vest with snap fasteners under the buttons.

Pants

To make and also to insert zipper (see Working Details). Leave 6½ inch opening for zipper at center front. Fold waistband in half, right sides together. Stitch a point at one end, straight across the other. Turn right side out and press. Place pointed end to center front opening at right side and stitch one layer to waist, straight end extending to form wrap. Slip stitch waistband inside. Fasten with hooks and eyes. Stitch pants hems.

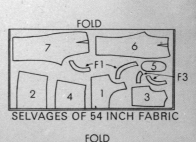

FOLD

SELVAGES OF 54 INCH FABRIC

FOLD

SELVAGES OF 48 INCH FABRIC

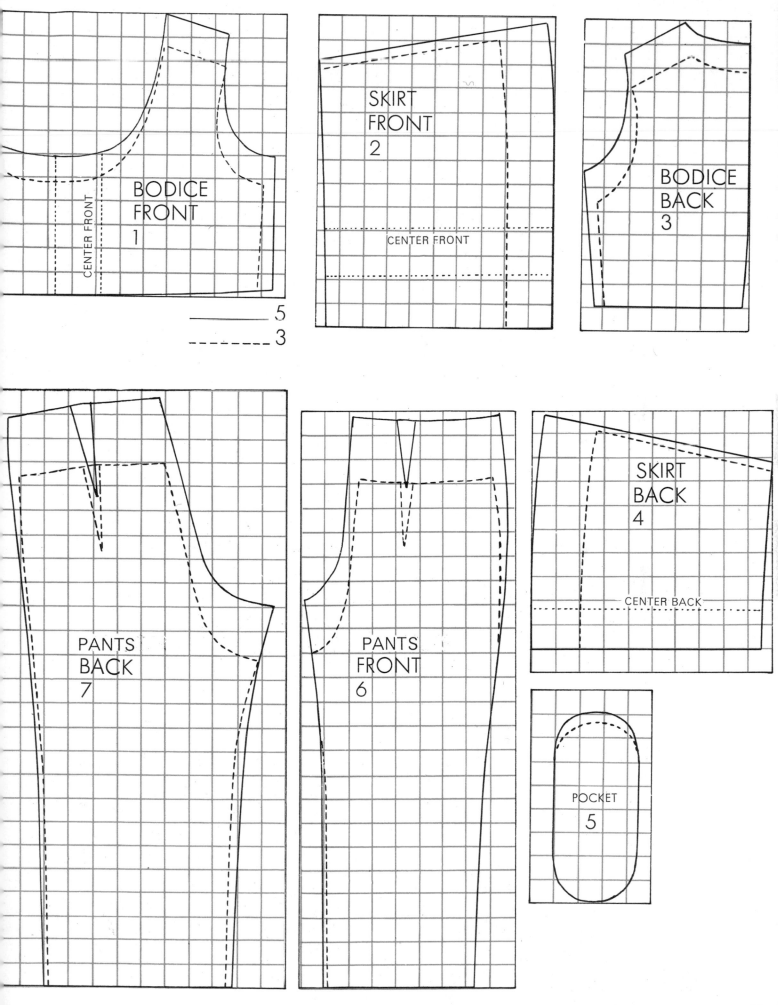

BODICE
FRONT
1

CENTER FRONT

——————— 5
- - - - - - 3

SKIRT
FRONT
2

CENTER FRONT

BODICE
BACK
3

PANTS
BACK
7

PANTS
FRONT
6

SKIRT
BACK
4

CENTER BACK

POCKET
5

9

Pretty dress with frilly sleeves, and single or double frilled hem

Fabric required

Sizes	3	5	7	yrs
Version A (left)				
Version B (right)				
36 inch fabric				
Version A & B	2¼	2⅜	2½	yds
48 inch fabric				
Version A & B	1¾	2	2	yds
Bias binding				
Version A	6½	6½	6½	yds
Version B	8	8	8	yds
Zipper	12	14	14	ins

To make pattern

See Know-how, also for patterns for neck facings.

To cut out

See Know-how. Fold 36 inch and 48 inch fabric lengthwise for pieces Nos. 1, 2, 7 and neck facings. Open out fabric and mark out the double width for frills Nos. 3, 4 and 5. *Remember to add turnings* to all pattern pieces except bound edges of frills. Cut frill patterns twice from single fabric. *Note:* pieces Nos. 4 and 6 are only needed for Version B.

Making dress
Version A

Stitch darts. Stitch shoulder, side and sleeve seams. Stitch center back seam from lower edge to within 12½ inches of neck edge for Size 3 years and to within 14½ inches for Sizes 5 and 7 years. Press. Stitch neck facings (see Working Details). Insert zipper in center back opening (see Working Details). Turn under ends of facing and slip stitch to zipper tape. Stitch sleeves into armholes (see Working Details). Stitch seams in sleeve frills. Press. Bind lower edges with bias binding (see Working Details). Gather top of frills to fit sleeves. With right sides together stitch frills to sleeves. Press turnings into sleeves. Cover seams on right sides with bias binding. Stitch seams in skirt frills to form circle. Press. Bind lower edge with bias binding. Gather top of frill to fit lower edge of skirt. With right sides facing, stitch frill to skirt, matching seams. Trim as for sleeves.

Version B

Make up as for Version A. Stitch seams of second skirt frill and bind lower edge with bias binding. Gather top frill to fit lower edge of skirt. Baste gathered edges of both frills together and stitch to dress. Trim as for Version A.

Remember—each square equals one inch square.

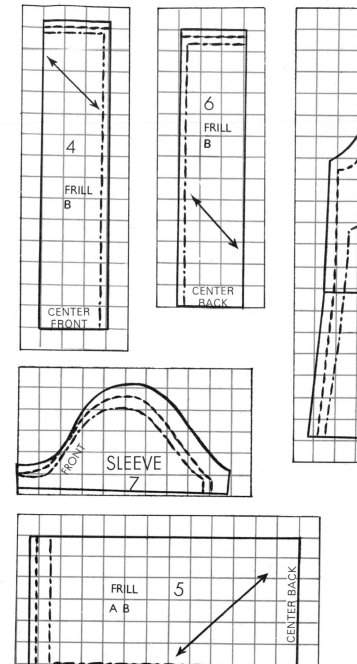

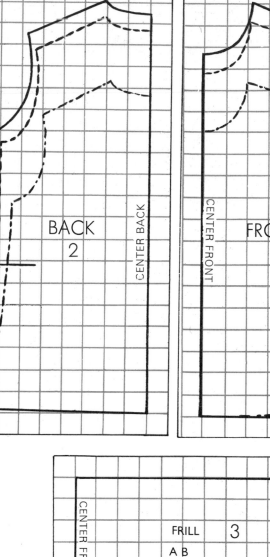

4
FRILL
B
CENTER FRONT

6
FRILL
B
CENTER BACK

BACK
2
CENTER BACK

CENTER FRONT
FRONT
1

SLEEVE
7
FRONT

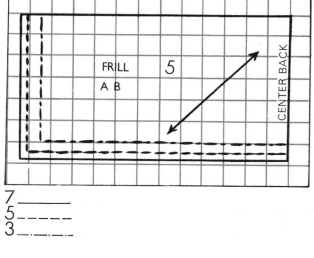

FRILL
5
A B
CENTER BACK

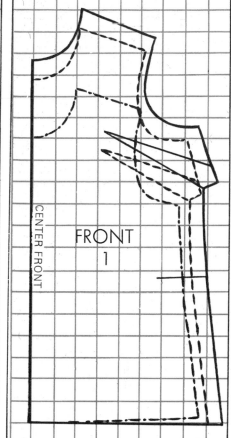

CENTER FRONT
FRILL
3
A B

7 ———
5 - - - -
3 -·-·-·

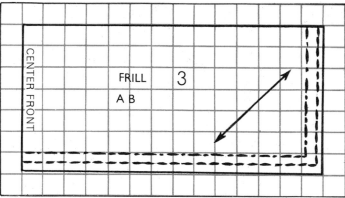

SLEEVE FRILL 8

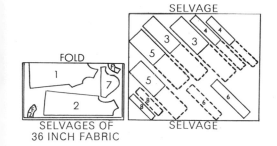

SELVAGE
FOLD
1
7
2
SELVAGES OF
36 INCH FABRIC

3   3
5
5

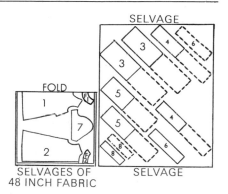

SELVAGE
3
3
5
5

FOLD
1
7
2
SELVAGES OF
48 INCH FABRIC
SELVAGE

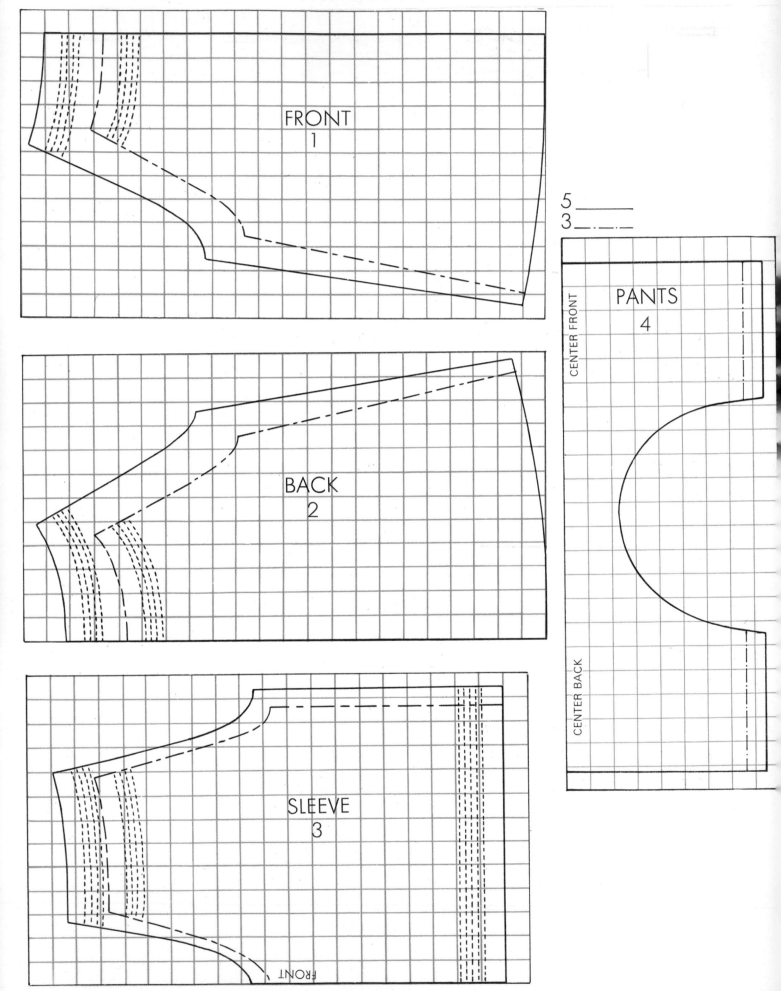

FRONT
1

BACK
2

SLEEVE
3

FRONT

PANTS
4

CENTER FRONT

CENTER BACK

5 _____
3 _ · _ · _

10

*Fresh, adaptable
angel top with elasticized
neck and sleeves.
Matching panties complete
the outfit*

Fabric required

Sizes	3	5	yrs
36 inch fabric	1⅝	1¾	yds
1 spool shirring elastic			

To make pattern
See Know-how.

To cut out
See Know-how. *Remember to add turnings and
hem allowances.*

Making the angel top
Join sleeves to bodice back and front with
French seams. Make narrow hems at neck
and wrists. Shir four rows of elastic at neck
and five rows at wrists as indicated on
pattern (see Working Details). Join underarm seams from wrist to armhole, then
through to hem with French seams. Turn
up hem and slip stitch into place.

Matching Panties
This pattern is optional. Allow ⅔ yd extra
material and place pattern piece on fold as
shown.
See Working Details for making up panties.
Remember—each square equals one inch square.

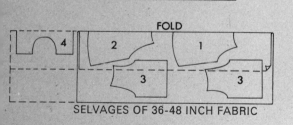

FOLD

SELVAGES OF 36-48 INCH FABRIC

11

Blouse and jumper dress

Fabric required

Sizes	3	5	7	yrs
Blouse				
36 inch fabric	1¼	1⅜	1½	yds
48 inch fabric	⅞	1	1⅛	yds
1 inch wide lace	1¼	1¼	1¼	yds
¼ inch wide elastic	½	⅞	½	yd
Buttons	5	5	5	
Jumper dress				
36 inch fabric	1⅜	1½	1¾	yds
48 inch fabric	¾	⅞	1	yd
Cord for lacing	1½	1½	1½	yds

To make pattern

See Know-how, also for neck facings for blouse, neck and armhole facings for jumper dress. Jumper neck facing to join fold-back front bodice facing.

To cut out

See Know-how. For jumper dress in 48 inch fabric, fold with selvages meeting. Pin pieces Nos. 4, 5, 6, 7 and F5 to folds. *Remember to add turnings and hem allowances.*

Making the blouse and dress

Blouse

Stitch front darts. Stitch shoulder, side and sleeve seams. Press. Stitch neck facings (see Working Details). Fold center back facings to inside and baste. Stitch blouse hem, opening out facing at lower edge. Slip stitch facing in place. Make five vertical buttonholes on right back (see Working Details), sew on buttons to correspond. Stitch sleeves into armholes (see Working Details). Stitch ½ inch hems on lower edges of sleeves for elastic casing, leaving opening for elastic. Sew lace to lower edges, on right side, with small running or back stitches. Insert elastic into casing to fit child's wrist. Fasten securely and close opening. Gather remaining lace and sew to neck edge.

Jumper dress

Stitch front darts. Stitch shoulder and side seams of bodice, side seams of skirt. Press. Stitch neck and sleeve facings (see Working Details). Fold back front facings and slip stitch to neck edge. Join bodice to skirt. Press. Make four evenly spaced eyelet holes, ½ inch from fold on each front. Turn up hem and slip stitch into place. Thread cord through eyelet holes.

Remember—each square equals one inch square.

BLOUSE
FRONT
1

CENTER FRONT

FRONT

BLOUSE
SLEEVE
3

CENTER FRONT

SKIRT
FRONT
6

SKIRT
BACK
7

CENTER BACK

7 ————
5 — — — —
3 —·—·—·

BLOUSE
BACK
2

BODICE
FRONT 4

BODICE
BACK
5

CENTER BACK

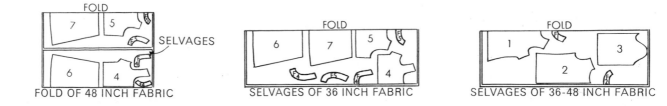

FOLD

7   5

SELVAGES

6   4

FOLD OF 48 INCH FABRIC

FOLD

6   7   5

4

SELVAGES OF 36 INCH FABRIC

FOLD

1   3

2

SELVAGES OF 36-48 INCH FABRIC

12

Long, warm nightgown; the gathered neck and cuffs are trimmed with bows

Fabric required

Sizes	3	5	7	yrs
36 inch fabric	2¾	3	3¼	yds
Bias binding	4	4	4	yds

To make pattern

See Know-how.

To cut out

See Know-how. *Remember to add turnings and hem allowances.* Cut piece No. 4 in single fabric.

Making the nightgown

Stitch sleeves to back and front with French seams (see Working Details). Stitch center back seam to within 6 inches of neck edge. Hem edges of center back opening. Press. Join sides and sleeves with French seams. Press. Fold collar frill lengthwise, right sides together and stitch across short ends. Turn to right side. Press. Attach frill as for collar (see Working Details). Gather neck to fit child with two rows of gathers. Cover seam on right side with bias binding, leaving tie ends at center back. Finish tie ends. Baste seams on curved pocket edges to wrong sides. Turn in pockets along top dotted line. Gather along lower dotted line and draw up to 4 inches. Stitch bias binding over gathers and trim with small bow. Stitch pockets to nightgown. Turn up 1¼ inch sleeve hems. Gather sleeves 1 inch above fold to fit child's wrist, but allowing hand to slip through without an opening. Trim sleeves with bows. Turn up hem and slip stitch into place.
Remember—each square equals one inch square.

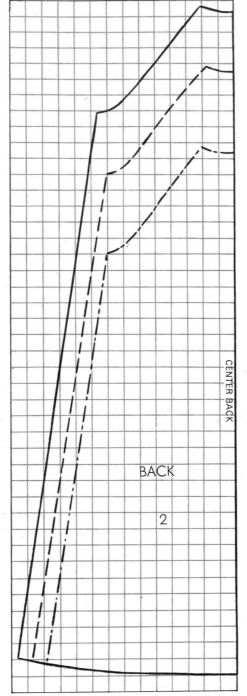
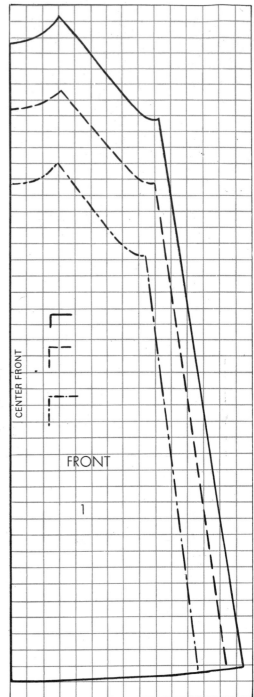
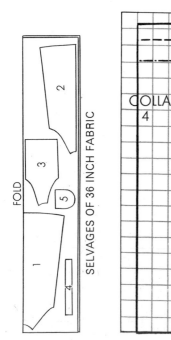
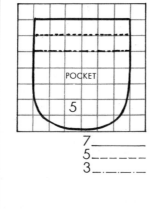
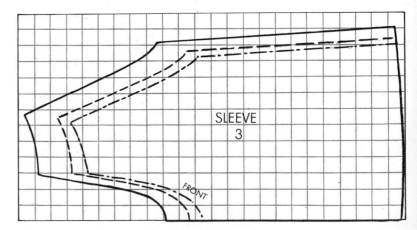

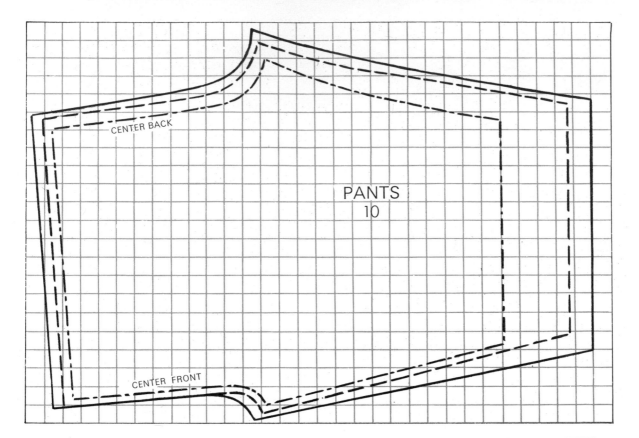

PANTS
10

CENTER BACK

CENTER FRONT

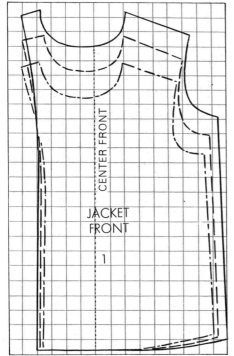

JACKET
FRONT

CENTER FRONT

1

JACKET
BACK
2

CENTER BACK

COLLAR
5
BACK

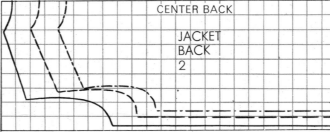

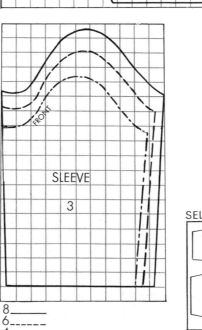

SLEEVE

3

FRONT

8 ————
6 - - - - - -
4 -·-·-·-

POCKET
6

SELVAGES

3

5

10

FOLD

2

6

1

SELVAGES   SELVAGES OF 36 INCH FABRIC

28

13

Pajamas with elasticized waist, bound pocket, collar and pants edges

Fabric required

Sizes	4	6	8	yrs
36 inch fabric	2¾	3⅛	3¼	yds
Buttons	4	4	4	
⅜ inch wide				
Elastic	1	1	1	yd
Binding	1½	1½	1½	yd

To make pattern
See Know-how.

To cut out
See Know-how. Fold fabric widthwise and place pieces Nos. 3, 5 and 10 as shown, turning over piece No. 5 and marking around again. *Remember to add turnings and hem allowances.*

Making the pajamas
Jacket
Use flat fell seams for all main sections. Stitch side and shoulder seams, easing back onto front. Stitch collar, (see Working Details, bind front edges and attach as for collar with revers). Stitch seams of sleeves. Stitch sleeves into armholes (see Working Details). Turn up and stitch sleeve hem. Open out front facings, turn up hem and slip stitch in place. Slip stitch facings in place. Make four evenly spaced buttonholes in left front (see Working Details). Sew buttons to correspond. Bind pocket tops. Fold turnings to inside on remaining edges of pockets. Pin and baste to jacket. Edge stitch in place.

Pants
See Working Details, making up pants. Fold in 1¼ inches at waist. Baste at fold. Turn under inner edge and stitch, leaving opening to insert elastic. Cut elastic to fit child comfortably, thread through casing and secure ends. Slip stitch opening closed. Turn up and stitch pants hem. Trim with binding.
Remember—each square equals one inch square.

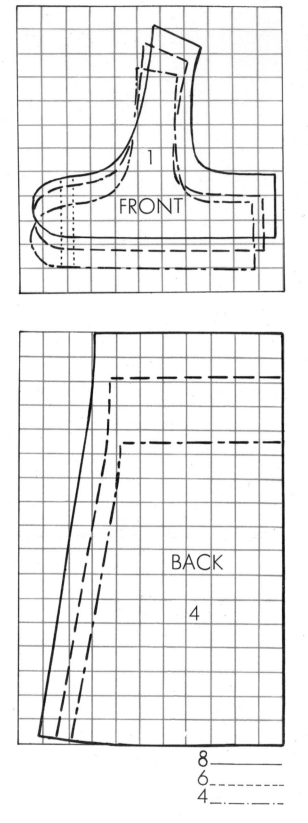

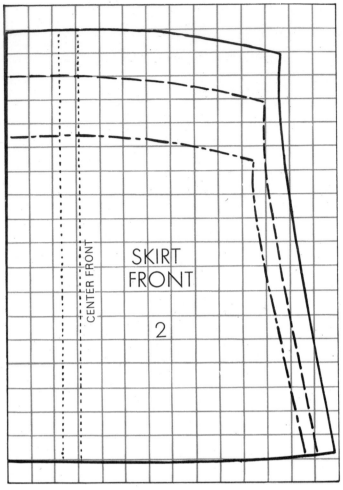

1

FRONT

SKIRT
FRONT

2

CENTER FRONT

BACK

4

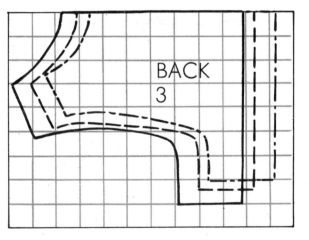

BACK
3

8 ——————
6 — — — —
4 —··—··—··

FOLD

4

3

3

1

1

2

SELVAGES OF
48-54 INCH FABRIC

FOLD

1

3

SELVAGES OF
36 INCH LINING

*Button-down jumper
dress, top-stitched
around the bodice
and shoulders*

Fabric required

Sizes	4	6	8	yrs
48 inch fabric	$\frac{7}{8}$	$1\frac{1}{8}$	$1\frac{3}{8}$	yds
54 inch fabric	$\frac{7}{8}$	1	$1\frac{1}{8}$	yds
36 inch lining	$\frac{3}{8}$	$\frac{3}{8}$	$\frac{3}{8}$	yd
Buttons	6	6	6	

To make pattern

See Know-how.

To cut out

See Know-how. *Remember to add turnings and
hem allowances.*

Making the dress

Stitch center back seam in lining, shoulder
seams in bodice and lining. Press. Place the
two layers, right sides together, and stitch
around armholes and from lower edge of
tab, starting at dotted line, around neck
edge to dotted line at lower edge of opposite
tab. Turn to right side and press carefully.
Stitch side seams of bodice and skirt. Press
skirt facings inside. Join bodice to skirt,
matching seams. Slip stitch facings in place
inside. Press. Topstitch bodice all around,
$\frac{3}{8}$ inch in from edges. Work six buttonholes
on right front, 2 inches apart for Size 4,
$2\frac{1}{2}$ inches for Size 6 and 3 inches apart for
Size 8 years, making first buttonhole in
center of tab (see Working Details). Sew on
buttons to correspond. Turn up hem.
Remember—each square equals one inch square.

15

Simple, well-shaped sleeveless dress with a butterfly motif

Fabric required

Sizes	4	6	yrs
36 inch fabric	$1\frac{3}{8}$	$1\frac{1}{2}$	yds
48 inch fabric	$\frac{3}{4}$	$\frac{7}{8}$	yd
Zipper	12	12	ins

To make pattern

See Know-how, also for pattern for armhole facing.

To cut out

See Know-how. Cut pieces Nos. 3 and 4 twice in double fabric. On 48 inch fabric fold piece No. 3 over and mark out the full shape before cutting out. *Remember to add turnings and hem allowances.*

Making the dress

Stitch shoulder seams of dress and both layers of neckband. Press. Place wrong side of upper neck band to right side of dress, matching shoulder seams. Pin and baste around neck edge. Turn in lower edge of facing and slip stitch or top stitch into place. Stitch side seams and center back seam to within $12\frac{1}{2}$ inches of neck edge. Press. Insert zipper in back opening (see Working Details). Stitch second neck band to form facing and stitch armhole facings (see Working Details). Turn up hem and slip stitch into place. Embroider a boldly colored butterfly in chain stitch or trim with a ready-made appliqué, slip stitch in place or use zigzag stitch.

Remember—each square equals one inch square.

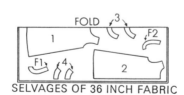

SELVAGES OF 36 INCH FABRIC

SELVAGES OF
48 INCH FABRIC

16

Puff-sleeved dress with a front insert trimmed with lace

Fabric required

Sizes	7	10	yrs
36 inch fabric			
or			
48 inch fabric	$1\frac{7}{8}$	$2\frac{1}{8}$	yds
Narrow lace	$5\frac{1}{2}$	$5\frac{1}{2}$	yds
Zipper	14	16	ins

To make pattern

See Know-how, also for patterns for neck facings.

To cut out

See Know-how. Open fabric out to cut pieces Nos. 4 and 5 twice, turn sleeve pattern around to cut a pair. *Remember to add turnings and hem allowances.*

Making the dress

Gather top of skirt front and draw up to fit lower edge of front insert. Adjust gathers evenly. With right sides together stitch insert to front. Snip into corners and press. Stitch side and shoulder seams, easing back onto front. Stitch center back seam from lower edge to within $14\frac{1}{2}$ inches of neck edge for Size 7 and $16\frac{1}{2}$ inches for Size 10 years. Press. Stitch neck facings (see Working Details). Insert zipper in center back opening (see Working Details). Stitch seams of sleeves and sleeve bands. Press. Make two rows of gathers on lower edges of sleeves to fit bands. With right sides together, matching seams, pin one edge of band to sleeve, adjusting gathers evenly. Stitch. Fold under remaining edge of sleeve band and slip stitch over previous line of stitching. Stitch sleeves into armholes (see Working Details). Turn up hem and slip stitch into place. Trim insert and around back and front neck with evenly spaced rows of lace as pictured, placing first row over seamline. Use fine needle and thread and small backstitch.

Remember—each square equals one inch square.

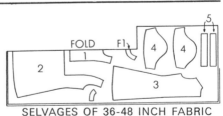

SELVAGES OF 36-48 INCH FABRIC

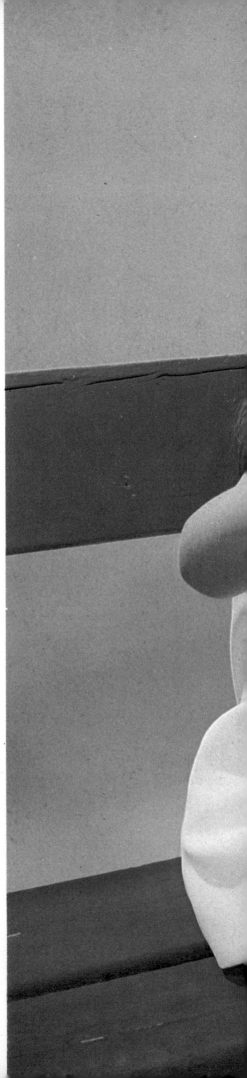

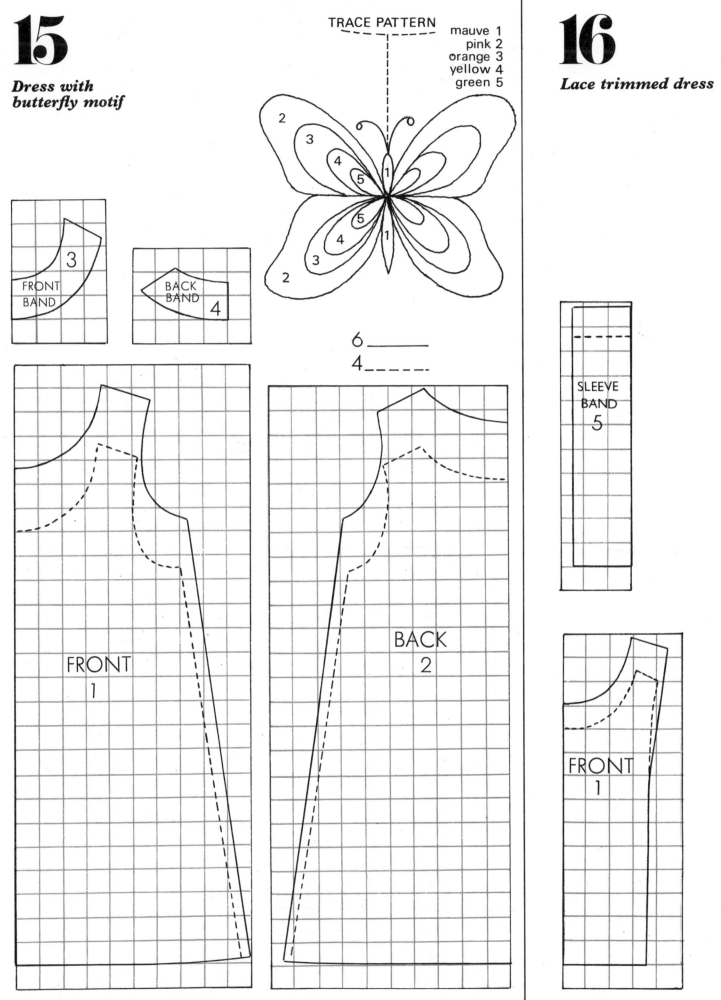

15

Dress with butterfly motif

TRACE PATTERN

mauve 1
pink 2
orange 3
yellow 4
green 5

16

Lace trimmed dress

3
FRONT
BAND

BACK
BAND
4

6 _____
4 _ _ _ _ _

SLEEVE
BAND
5

FRONT
1

BACK
2

FRONT
1

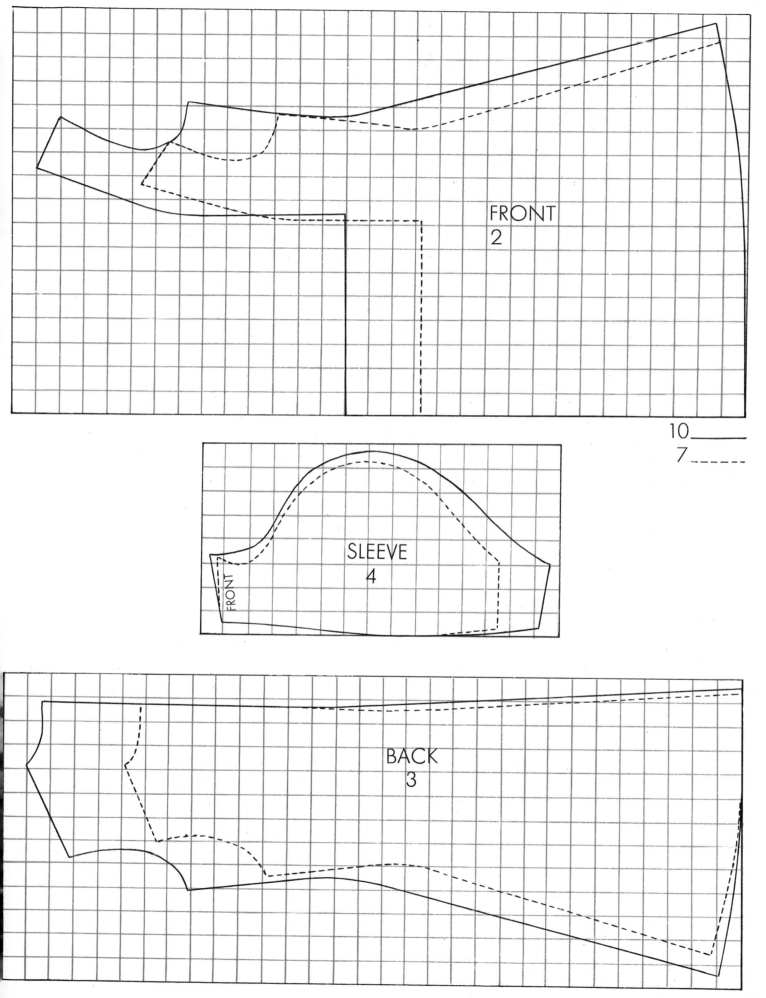

FRONT
2

10 _____
7 - - - - -

SLEEVE
4

FRONT

BACK
3

17

Sleeveless dress with contrasting tab front and pockets

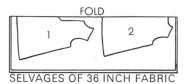

FOLD

1   2

SELVAGES OF 36 INCH FABRIC

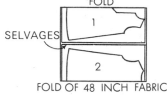

FOLD

SELVAGES

1

2

FOLD OF 48 INCH FABRIC

FOLD   4

3

5

SELVAGES OF 36-48 INCH FABRIC

Fabric required

Sizes	2	4	6	yrs
36 inch fabric	$1\frac{5}{8}$	$1\frac{5}{8}$	$1\frac{3}{4}$	yds
48 inch fabric	$\frac{3}{4}$	$\frac{7}{8}$	$\frac{7}{8}$	yd
Contrasting fabric	$\frac{1}{4}$	$\frac{1}{4}$	$\frac{1}{4}$	yd
Bias binding	1	1	1	yd
Small button	1	1	1	

To make pattern
See Know-how.

To cut out
See Know-how. Fold 48 inch fabric in with selvages meeting. *Remember to add turnings and hem allowances.*

Making the dress
Stitch shoulder and side seams. Press. Bind armhole edges with bias binding (see Working Details). With right sides facing, stitch shoulder seams in both layers of contrasting neck and front bands. With right sides facing, stitch neck and front edges of bands together. Trim and clip into turnings where necessary. Turn band right side out and press. Fold under raw edges of band, clip turnings at angles. Press. Clip into turning at center front point of dress. Sandwich neck and front edges of dress between turned-in edges of band, carefully matching edges at point. Edge stitch in place. On wrong side slip stitch edges of band together for $\frac{1}{2}$ inch near point to strengthen. Fasten neck with button and loop. Fold pockets in half, right sides together. Stitch side and lower edges, leaving space for turning. Turn right side out. Press and stitch in place. Turn up hem, slip stitch in place.

Remember—each square equals one inch square.

18

Dress with collar, shoulder inserts and buttonhole band in contrasting fabric

FOLD

2   1

F2   F1

SELVAGES OF 36 INCH FABRIC

FOLD

2

1

F2

F1

FOLD OF 48 INCH FABRIC

6   FOLD

5

4

3

SELVAGES OF 36-48 INCH FABRIC

Fabric required

Sizes	5	7	9	yrs
36 inch fabric	$1\frac{5}{8}$	$1\frac{7}{8}$	2	yds
48 inch fabric	$\frac{7}{8}$	1	1	yd
Contrasting fabric	$\frac{1}{2}$	$\frac{1}{2}$	$\frac{1}{2}$	yd
Buttons	6	6	6	

To make pattern
See Know-how, also for pattern for armhole facing.

To cut out
See Know-how. Fold 48 inch fabric in with selvages meeting. *Remember to add turnings and hem allowances.*

Making the dress
On front and back shoulder contrast pieces fold turnings of lower curved edges to inside and baste. Place on front and back of dress and baste in position at armhole, shoulder and neck edges. Edge stitch along lower curves. Stitch shoulder and side seams. Press. Stitch facings to armholes (see Working Details). Snip diagonally into lower corners of front opening. Make neat across lower edge of opening. With right sides together, fold front band lengthwise along fold line. Stitch across lower edge and turn to right side. With right sides together, raw edge of narrower side of band to opening, stitch band to opening. Press turnings open. Slip stitch other edge of band inside. With left hand band underneath, right hand band on top and lower edge of opening sandwiched between, slip stitch lower edge of band to dress. Stitch front and smaller curved edges of neckbands. Turn to right side (see Working Details, making collar). Starting at neckband, make six buttonholes on right side of front. Sew buttons to correspond. Hem lower edge.

Remember—each square equals one inch square.

17

Sleeveless dress with contrasting tab front

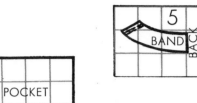

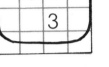

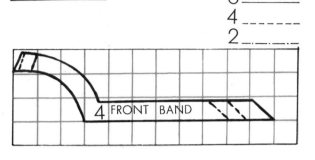

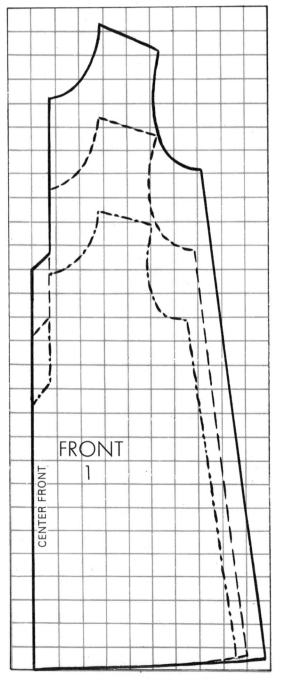

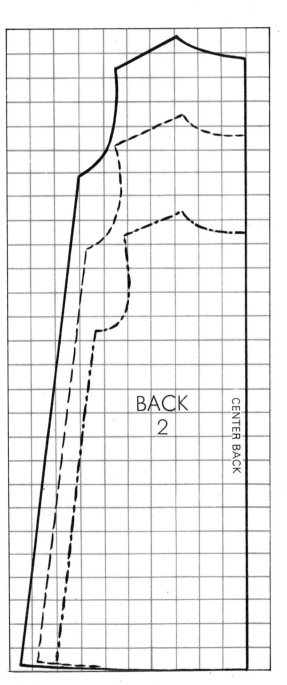

18

Dracess with contrasting tab and shoulder inserts

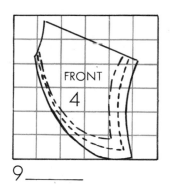

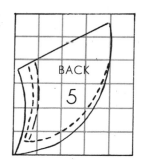

FRONT
4

BACK
5

9 ——————
7 — — — — —
5 —·—·—·—

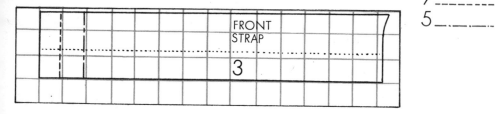

FRONT
STRAP
3

NECK BAND 6

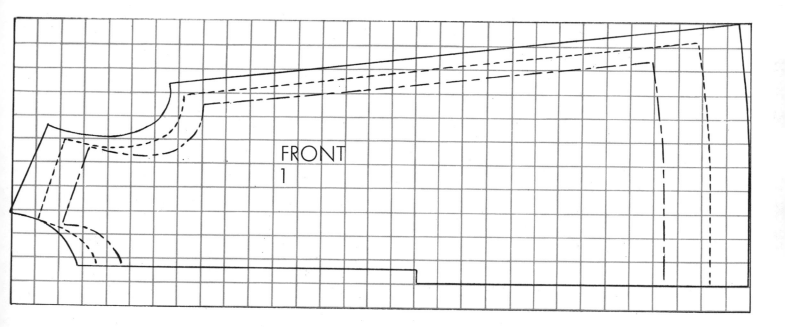

FRONT
1

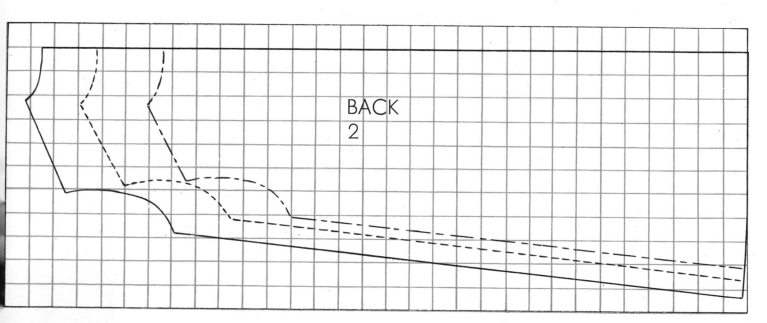

BACK
2

19

Low-waisted dress with a back zipper and double rows of lace on the collar and cuffs

Fabric required

Sizes	5	7	9	yrs
36 inch fabric	$1\frac{7}{8}$	$2\frac{1}{4}$	$2\frac{1}{2}$	yds
48 inch fabric	$1\frac{7}{8}$	2	$2\frac{1}{8}$	yds
$\frac{5}{8}$ inch wide lace	$4\frac{1}{2}$	$4\frac{1}{2}$	$4\frac{1}{2}$	yds
Zipper	14	15	16	ins

To make pattern

See Know-how, also for patterns for neck facings.

To cut out

See Know-how. *Remember to add turnings and hem allowances.*

Making the dress

Stitch shoulder seams, easing back onto front. Stitch side and sleeve seams. Press. Stitch center back seam from lower edge to within $14\frac{1}{2}$ inches of neck edge for Size 5, $15\frac{1}{2}$ inches for Size 7 and $16\frac{1}{2}$ inches for Size 9 years. Press. Stitch skirt to bodice, matching seams. Stitch neck facing (see Working Details). Insert zipper in center back opening (see Working Details). Stitch sleeves into armholes (see Working Details). Turn up and stitch skirt and sleeve hems. Measure twice length of sleeve hem. Cut off this amount of lace. Gather lace to fit sleeve. Stitch to right side, $\frac{1}{2}$ inch above sleeve edge using small running or back stitch. Sew another row $\frac{3}{8}$ inch above this. Repeat for neck and the other sleeve.
Remember—each square equals one inch square.

20

Shift dress with trumpet sleeves and a stand-up collar — both trimmed with lace

Fabric required

Sizes	6	8	10	yrs
36 inch fabric	2	$2\frac{1}{8}$	$2\frac{1}{4}$	yds
48 inch fabric	$1\frac{1}{4}$	$1\frac{3}{8}$	$1\frac{1}{2}$	yds
$\frac{3}{4}$ inch wide lace	$2\frac{1}{2}$	$2\frac{1}{2}$	$2\frac{3}{4}$	yds
Zipper	14	14	16	ins
2 hooks and eyes				

To make pattern

See Know-how.

To cut out

See Know-how. Cut neckband No. 3 from opened out single fabric. *Remember to add turnings and hem allowances.*

Making the dress

Stitch darts. Stitch shoulder, side and sleeve seams. Press. Stitch center back seam to within $14\frac{1}{2}$ inches of neck edge for Sizes 6 and 8 years and $16\frac{1}{2}$ inches for Size 10 years. Insert zipper into back opening (see Working Details). Stitch sleeves into armholes (see Working Details). Fold neckband in half, right sides together, stitch across short ends. Turn right side out and press. Turn up hems of dress and sleeves and slip stitch in place. Measure twice length of sleeve hem, cut off this amount of lace. Gather lace to fit sleeve. Stitch to right side with small running or back stitches. Repeat for other sleeve and neck frills. Fasten neck with two hooks and eyes.
Remember—each square equals one inch square.

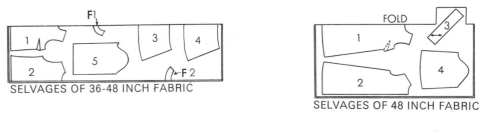

SELVAGES OF 36-48 INCH FABRIC

SELVAGES OF 48 INCH FABRIC

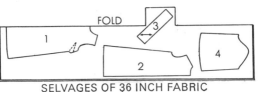

SELVAGES OF 36 INCH FABRIC

19

*Low-waisted dress
with lace trimmings*

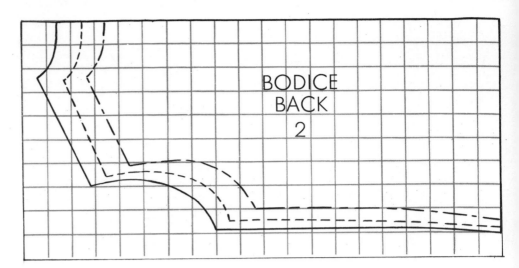

BODICE
BACK
2

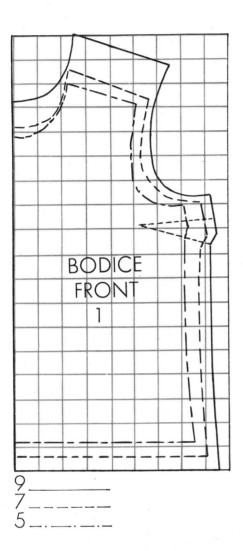

BODICE
FRONT
1

9 ———
7 – – –
5 –·–·–

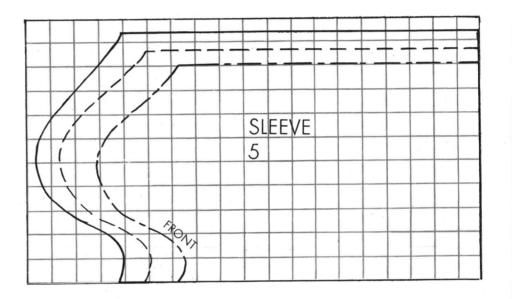

SLEEVE
5

FRONT

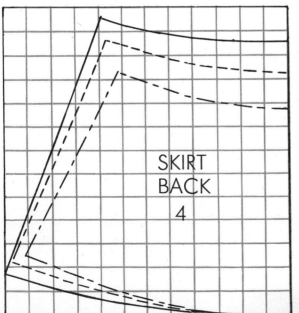

SKIRT
BACK
4

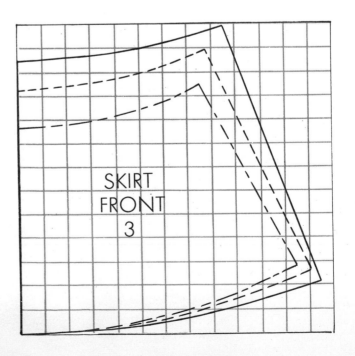

SKIRT
FRONT
3

20

**Shift dress with
trumpet sleeves**

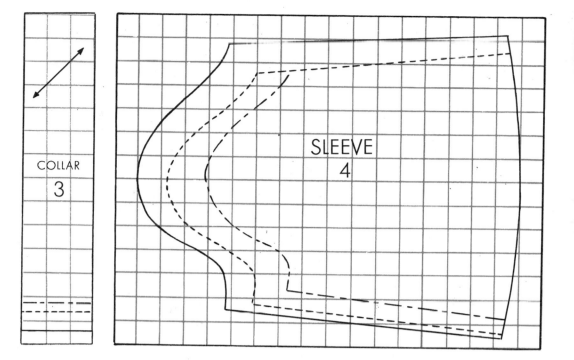

COLLAR
3

SLEEVE
4

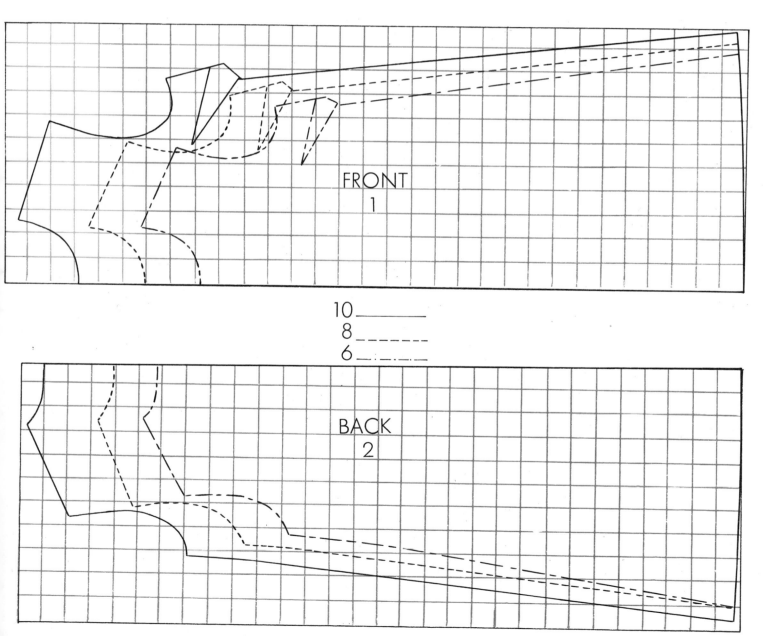

FRONT
1

10 _____
8 ─ ─ ─ ─
6 ─ · ─ · ─

BACK
2

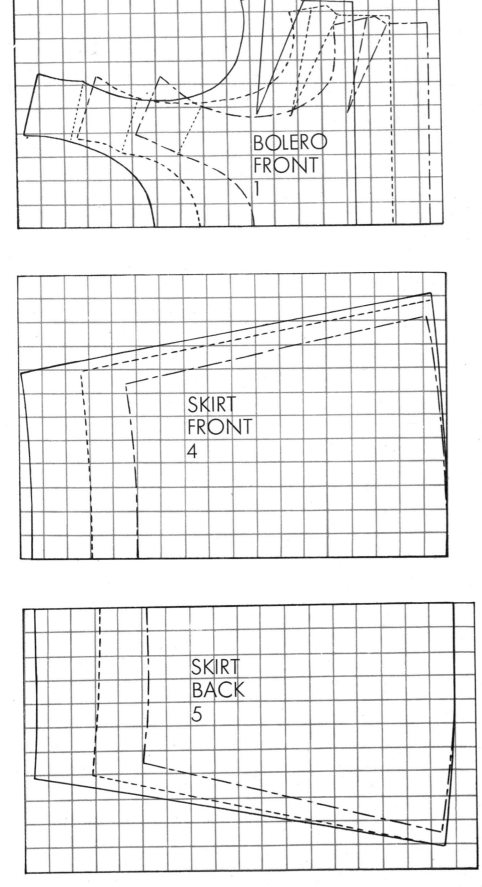

BOLERO
FRONT
1

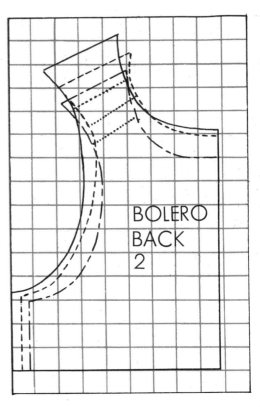

BOLERO
BACK
2

SKIRT
FRONT
4

SKIRT FRONT BAND
6

SKIRT BACK BAND
7

SKIRT
BACK
5

12 ——
10 - - - -
8 - · - ·

POCKET
3

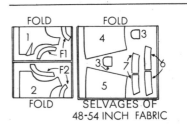

FOLD   FOLD

FOLD   SELVAGES OF
              48-54 INCH FABRIC

21

Tailored skirt and bolero. The top buttons across one shoulder and the skirt has a back zipper and button detail at the front

Fabric required

Sizes	8	10	12	yrs
48 inch fabric or				
54 inch fabric	1⅜	1⅜	1½	yds
Zipper	5	5	5	ins
Buttons	4	4	4	
Hook and eye				

To make pattern

See Know-how, also for patterns for neck and armhole facings (1¼ inches wide).

To cut out

See Know-how. Fold fabric with selvages meeting at center and place pieces Nos. 1 and 2 and facings as shown. Cut pieces Nos. 3, 6 and 7 twice in double fabric. *Remember to add turnings and hem allowances.*

Making the outfit

Bolero

Stitch darts and side seams. Press. Stitch neck and armhole facings (see Working Details). Turn in right front shoulder along fold line and baste. Make two vertical buttonholes in left front shoulder (see Working Details). Topstitch ¼ inch in around armhole, shoulder and neck edges. Wrap right front over back shoulder and slip stitch in place. Sew two buttons to left back shoulder. Turn up hem and slip stitch in place. With right sides together stitch pocket sections, leaving small opening to turn through. Press. Topstitch ¾ inch from top, then right around and slip stitch pocket to bolero.

Skirt

Stitch side seams of skirt and both layers of waistband. Press. With right sides facing stitch the two layers of waistbands together around top, front and lower edges, leaving center back edges open (waistband is still in two halves). Turn to right side and press. Topstitch along waist edge and around to center front on lower edge. Place left waistband over raw edge of skirt, centers and side seams matching and topstitch in place. Repeat with right waistband and topstitch as far as center front. Slip stitch both layers of band together at waist edge and trim with two buttons. Stitch center back seam to within 5½ inches of waist edge. Insert zipper in center back opening (see Working Details). Stitch hook and eye to fasten to top of waistband. Turn up hem and slip stitch in place. Take second pocket and slip stitch to right back of skirt.

Remember—each square equals one inch square.

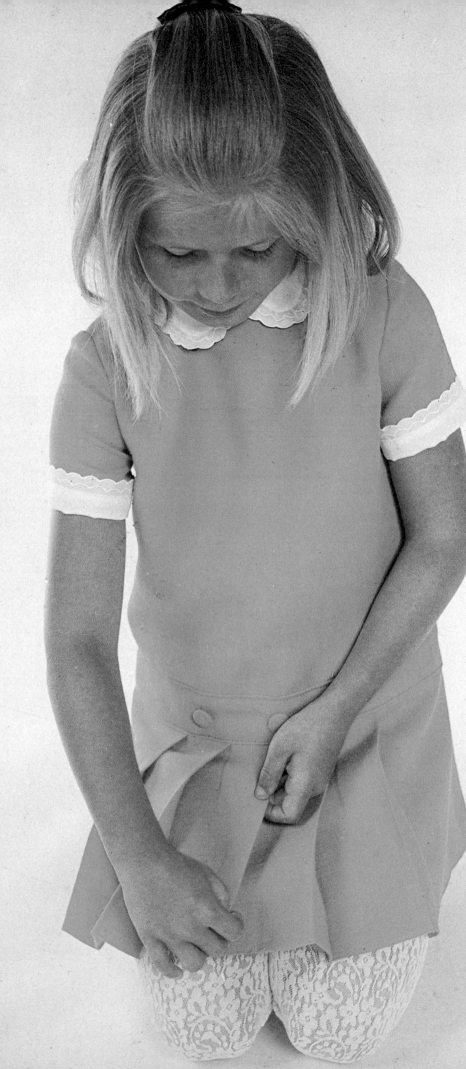

22

Dress with a dropped waist and front pleated skirt. The round collar and short sleeves are trimmed with lace

Fabric required

Sizes	6	8	10	yrs
48 inch fabric or				
54 inch fabric	$1\frac{1}{8}$	$1\frac{1}{4}$	$1\frac{3}{8}$	yds
Fabric for collar and cuffs	$\frac{1}{4}$	$\frac{1}{4}$	$\frac{1}{4}$	yd
Frilling	$1\frac{1}{4}$	$1\frac{1}{4}$	$1\frac{1}{4}$	yds
Zipper	16	17	19	ins
Buttons	3	3	3	

To make pattern
See Know-how

To cut out
See Know-how. Open out fabric to cut front skirt. *Remember to add turnings and hem allowances,* (2 inch hem only).

Making the dress
Stitch shoulder and side seams of bodice, side seams of skirt. Press. Make skirt hem. Stitch side seams of front and back hip insets. On front skirt, fold in pleats, placing crosses onto adjacent dots (see Working Details, making pleats). With right sides together, matching side seams, stitch lower edge of one hip band to top edge of skirt, then stitch skirt and band to bodice. Fold under raw edges of second hip band and slip stitch in place inside to make raw edges neat. Top-stitch $\frac{1}{4}$ inch from both edges of hip band. Stitch center back seam from lower edge to within $16\frac{1}{2}$ inches of neck edge for Size 6, $17\frac{1}{2}$ inches for Size 8 and $19\frac{1}{2}$ inches for Size 10 years. Insert zipper in center back opening (see Working Details). With right sides together, inserting frilling so that raw edges lie together, stitch outer edges of two collar sections. Repeat for second half of collar (see Working Details, making collar). Stitch side seams of sleeves and cuffs. With right sides together, inserting frilling as for collar, stitch cuffs to sleeves. Fold cuffs in half to wrong side and slip stitch in place. Stitch sleeves into armholes (see Working Details). Sew buttons to front.
Remember—each square equals one inch square.

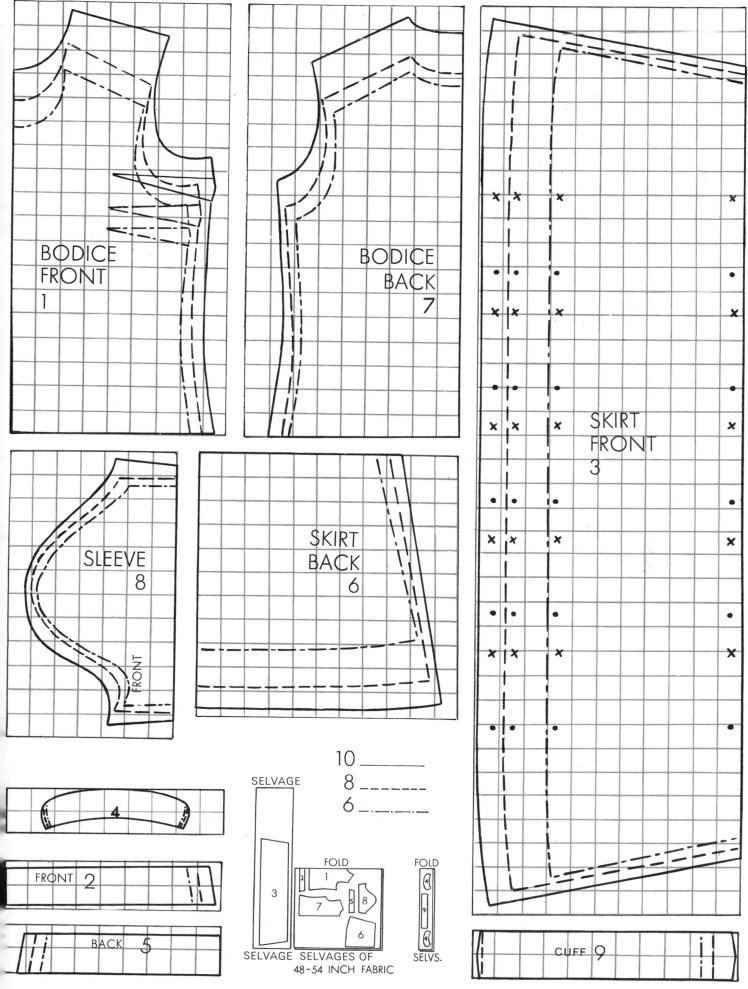

BODICE
FRONT
1

BODICE
BACK
7

SLEEVE
8

FRONT

SKIRT
BACK
6

SKIRT
FRONT
3

4

FRONT 2

BACK 5

SELVAGE

10 ——————
8 – – – – – –
6 –·–·–·–·

SELVAGE   SELVAGES OF
48-54 INCH FABRIC

FOLD

3

2   1

7   5   8

6

FOLD

4

9

4

SELVS.

CUFF 9

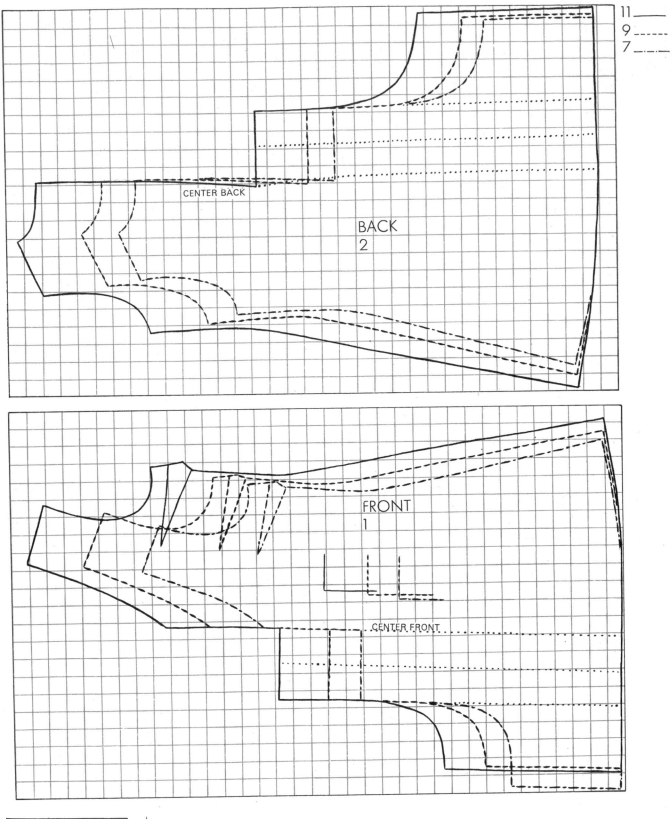

11 ⎯⎯⎯
9 – – –
7 —·—·

CENTER BACK

BACK
2

FRONT
1

CENTER FRONT

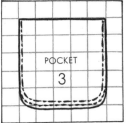

POCKET
3

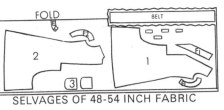

FOLD

BELT

2

1

SELVAGES OF 48-54 INCH FABRIC

23

Beautifully cut culotte dress, the front edges are top-stitched to give a crisp finish

Fabric required

Sizes	7	9	11	yrs
48 inch fabric				
or				
54 inch fabric	1¾	1⅞	2⅛	yds
Buckle	1	1	1	
Zipper	8	10	10	ins

To make pattern

See Know-how, also for neck and armhole facings.

To cut out

See Know-how. *Remember to add turnings.* Add 2 inches for hem. For belt, cut strip 3¼ inches by 34 inches, for belt carriers, cut four strips, each 3¼ inches by 1¼ inches.

Making the culotte dress

Stitch darts. Stitch center back seam from neck to 4½ inches below pleat extension for Size 7 years and 6 inches for Sizes 9 and 11 years, following center back line. Stitch center front seam for 2 inches only, below zipper opening. Stitch shoulder seams. Press. Stitch neck facings (see Working Details). Baste zipper in center front opening (see Working Details). Baste and press center front and center back folds forming pleat edges. Topstitch ¼ inch from edge, around neck, either side of zipper and continuing down pleat edges. Topstitch back pleat edges. Stitch curved back and front center seams from 2 inches below pleat extension. Press. Form pleats in front and back as marked with dotted lines on diagram. Catch top edges of pleats together. Make neat open front edges. Stitch inner leg seams, stitching right through so that back joins front. Stitch side seams. Press. Stitch armhole facings (see Working Details). Hem leg edges. Fold belt carriers in three and top-stitch through center. Stitch two belt carriers to front and two to back waist. Make belt (see Working Details). With right sides together, stitch pocket sections in pairs, leaving small openings to turn through. Turn right side out, close openings, press and topstitch. Slip stitch in place on culottes.

Remember—each square equals one inch square.

Vest, suitable for either a boy or girl, shown here trimmed with a double row of braid

Fabric required

Sizes	7	9	11	yrs
48 inch fabric				
or				
54 inch fabric	$\frac{1}{2}$	$\frac{5}{8}$	$\frac{5}{8}$	yd
36 inch lining	$\frac{1}{2}$	$\frac{5}{8}$	$\frac{5}{8}$	yd
Plain braid	$3\frac{1}{8}$	$3\frac{1}{8}$	$3\frac{1}{8}$	yds
Fancy braid	$3\frac{1}{8}$	$3\frac{1}{8}$	$3\frac{1}{8}$	yds

To make pattern

See Know-how.

To cut out

See Know-how. If using plaid fabric be careful to match the plaid and treat fabric as one way. Add seam allowances at shoulders and side seams only.

Making the vest

Stitch darts, side and shoulder seams on vest and lining. Press. With wrong sides facing, slip stitch lining and vest together around neck, fronts, lower edge and armholes, taking care not to stretch bias edges. Fold and press plain braid so that one edge overlaps $\frac{1}{16}$ inch. Allowing enough braid to make flat seam joins at center back neck and underarms, topstitch braid in place, narrower side uppermost. Press edges. Topstitch second braid in place, covering previous stitching, easing around curved edges and making neat joins.

Remember—each square equals one inch square.

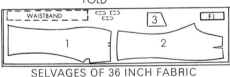

Impeccably shaped pants, adapted for either boy or girl

Fabric required

Sizes	7	9	11	yrs
36 inch fabric	$1\frac{5}{8}$	$1\frac{7}{8}$	$2\frac{1}{8}$	yds
54 inch fabric				
or				
60 inch fabric	$\frac{7}{8}$	1	$1\frac{1}{8}$	yds
Zipper	5	5	6	ins
Button	1	1	1	
Girl's pants				
$1\frac{1}{4}$ inch wide				
Belting ribbon	$\frac{1}{2}$	$\frac{1}{2}$	$\frac{1}{2}$	yd
$1\frac{1}{4}$ inch wide				
Elastic	$\frac{1}{2}$	$\frac{1}{2}$	$\frac{1}{2}$	yd

To make pattern

See Know-how.

To cut out

See Know-how. *Remember to add turnings and hem allowances.* Allow nothing around fly front extension. For waistband, cut strip $3\frac{1}{4}$ inches by $26\frac{1}{2}$ inches. For belt carriers cut five strips, each $1\frac{1}{4}$ inches by $2\frac{1}{4}$ inches. (For girl's pants omit belt carriers and pockets). For fly backing cut strip 2 inches by $6\frac{1}{2}$ inches.

Making the pants

Boy's pants

Turn under top edge of pockets and topstitch $\frac{3}{4}$ inch from edge. Pin pockets in place and topstitch close to edge, turning under $\frac{1}{4}$ inch. Make up pants (see Working Details) finishing front crotch seam at base of zipper opening. Nip through seam allowances at base of fly extension on both fronts. On right front, fold under fly extension 1 inch and placing opening of zipper $\frac{5}{8}$ inch from top edge, topstitch close to teeth. Place fly backing level with top and $1\frac{1}{4}$ inches beyond zipper and stitch in place through previous stitching line. Fold under left fly extension $1\frac{1}{4}$ inches, pin in place $\frac{1}{4}$ inch to right of closed zipper. Baste remaining loose side of zipper close to teeth. Keeping fly backing folded back, topstitch two rows, $\frac{3}{4}$ inch and 1 inch from left center to base of zipper only. Bring fly backing forward and continue two rows of topstitching for 1 inch below zipper. Fold waistband with one edge extending $\frac{1}{4}$ inch and close end seams. With right sides facing, pin extending edge of waistband to top edge of pants. Stitch. Turn waistband inside and topstitch $\frac{1}{8}$ inch from seamline, also $\frac{1}{8}$ inch from top edge. Fold belt carriers in three and topstitch through center. Stitch two in front and three at back of waist. Make buttonhole $\frac{1}{2}$ inch from left front edge of waistband (see Working Details). Sew button to correspond. Turn up hems. Press creases.

Girl's pants. As boy's, reversing fly. Topstitch front creases close to edge. Interline waistband with belting ribbon in front, secured to elastic at back side seams.

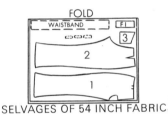

SELVAGES OF 54 INCH FABRIC.

SELVAGES OF 36 INCH FABRIC

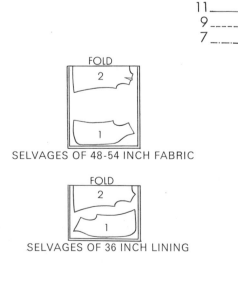

SELVAGES OF 48-54 INCH FABRIC

SELVAGES OF 36 INCH LINING

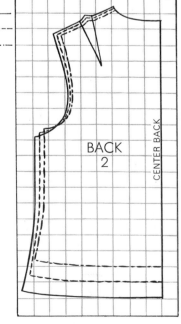

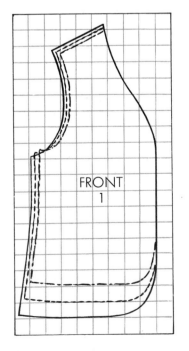

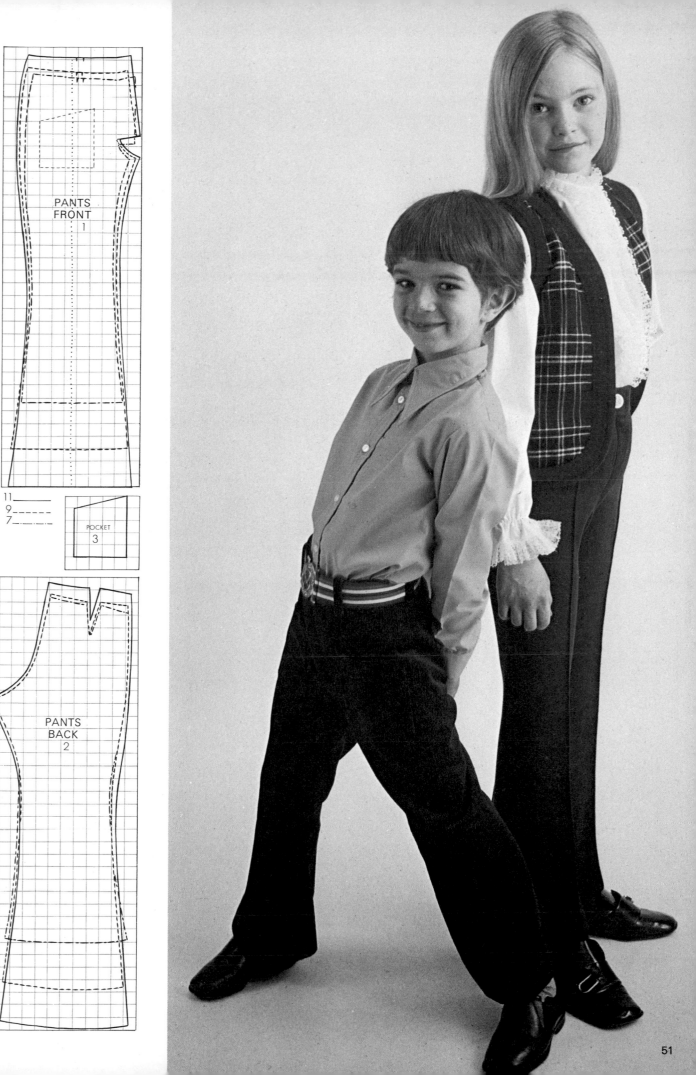

PANTS
FRONT
1

11 ————
9 - - - - -
7 —·—·—

POCKET
3

PANTS
BACK
2

26

Dress with a low roll collar, shirred waist and sleeve cuffs. The dress fastens with a back zipper

Fabric required

Sizes	7	9	11	yrs
36 inch fabric	2¼	2⅜	2⅝	yds
48 inch fabric	2⅛	2⅜	2½	yds
Zipper	14	14	16	ins

1 spool shirring elastic
2 hooks and eyes

To make pattern

See Know-how.

To cut out

See Know-how. Cut collar piece No. 5 in single fabric. *Remember to add turnings and hem allowances.*

Making the dress

Stitch side seams in skirt and press. Turn up sleeve hems, finish off edges and baste in place. Shir ten rows of elastic ⅜ inch apart across top of skirt and seven rows across lower edge of each sleeve, starting as near hem fold as possible (see Working Details). Stitch shoulder, side and sleeve seams. Press. Join bodice to skirt, easing skirt fullness evenly around bodice. Press. Stitch center back seam from lower edge to within 14½ inches of neck edge for Sizes 7 and 9 and 16½ inches for Size 11 years. Stitch sleeves into armholes (see Working Details). Insert zipper into center back opening, sew by hand over shirring, (see Working Details). Fold collar in half and stitch across short ends. Turn right side out and press (see Working Details, making collar). Fasten with two hooks and eyes. Turn up hem and slip stitch.

Remember—each square equals one inch square.

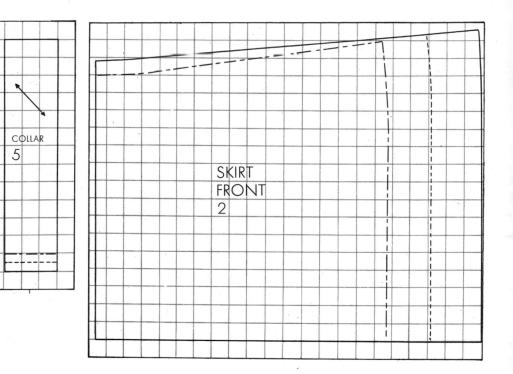

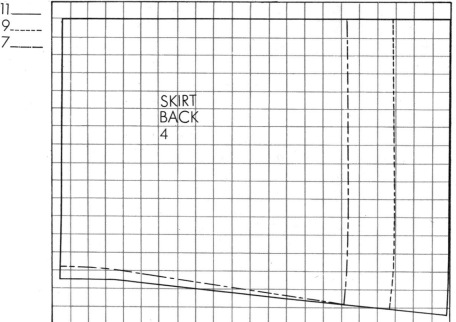

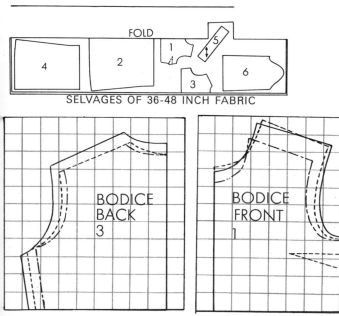

SELVAGES OF 36-48 INCH FABRIC

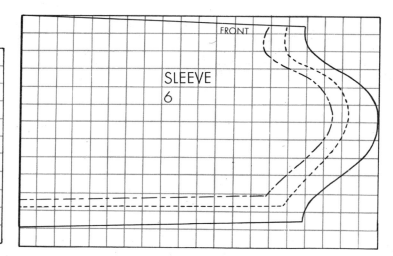

27

Dress and jacket — the dress zips up the back, fastening with a button at the neck. The jacket is low cut and buttons at the waist

Fabric required

Sizes	7	9	11	yrs
Dress				
48 inch fabric	1⅝	1¾	1⅞	yds
54 inch fabric	1¼	1⅜	1⅜	yds
Jacket				
48 inch fabric				
or				
54 inch fabric	½	½	½	yd
36 inch lining	½	½	½	yd
Zipper	12	14	15	ins
Buttons	5	5	5	

To make pattern

See Know-how, also for patterns for neck facings (1¼ inches wide).

To cut out

See Know-how. Cut pieces Nos. 4, 5 and 6 twice in double fabric. *Remember to add turnings and hem allowances (only ¾ inch on jacket).*

Making the outfit

Dress

Stitch darts, shoulder, side, sleeve and center back seams, also facing seams at shoulders. Press. Stitch center front seam from lower edge to within 12½ inches of neck tab for Size 7, 14½ inches for Size 9 and 15½ inches for Size 11 years. Press. Stitch sleeves into armholes (see Working Details). Stitch collar (see Working Details). Pin collar to neck, right sides together. Place facing on top, raw edges together and stitch from inner edge of tab on left side around to inner edge of tab on right side. Clip into angle of tabs and turn facing to wrong side. Press. Insert zipper in center front, (see Working Details). Slip stitch facings to zipper tape and shoulder seams. With right sides together, stitch tab sections in pairs, leaving openings to turn through. Turn right side out, close opening and topstitch ¼ inch from edge. Pin in position on right sides of pocket sections. Cover with second pocket section. Stitch together as for tabs. Topstitch in position, also around tab and collar edges. Work a buttonhole in right tab (see Working Details), sew button to correspond. Trim pockets with buttons. Stitch sleeve and dress hems.

Jacket

Stitch shoulder seams of jacket and lining. Press. Stitch lining and jacket together, right sides facing, around all edges except side seams. Turn to right side. Stitch side seams of jacket, leaving lining loose. Press. Slip stitch side seams of lining together. Topstitch ¼ inch from all edges. Work two buttonholes in right front, sew on buttons. *Remember—each square equals one inch square.*

FOLD

SELVAGES OF
48-54 INCH FABRIC
AND
36 INCH LINING

FOLD

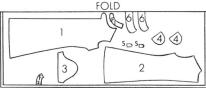
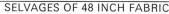

SELVAGES OF 48 INCH FABRIC

FOLD

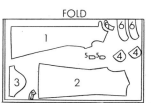

SELVAGES OF 54 INCH FABRIC

28

Front-buttoned dress with a dropped waist and two pockets on the skirt. The collar, tab front, pocket and waist seams are top-stitched

Fabric required

Sizes	8	10	12	yrs
48 inch fabric				
or				
54 inch fabric	1½	1⅝	1¾	yds
Buttons	7	7	7	

To make pattern

See Know-how.

To cut out

See Know-how. Open out fabric to full width. Fold over pattern pieces Nos. 2, 3, 4 and 8 and mark out complete pattern shapes. Cut pieces Nos. 1, 5 and 8 twice in single fabric, turning the pieces over to make pairs. Cut pocket piece No. 7 four times. *Remember to add turnings and hem allowances.*

Making the dress

Stitch darts, shoulder and sleeve seams, bodice and skirt side seams. Press. Fold front facings to right side and stitch from fold across neckline for 1½ inches. Turn to wrong side. Stitch sleeves into armholes (see Working Details). Wrap right front over left, matching centers. Join bodice to skirt. Press. Fold under turnings on front band, baste and press. Topstitch band to right bodice front as far as skirt seam. Break stitching and start again below seam, stitching band to skirt. Continue topstitching around waist. Slip stitch inner and neck edge of band to bodice. Make five evenly spaced vertical buttonholes in center of band (see Working Details). Stitch collar (see Working Details), topstitching outer edges. Stitch pocket sections together in pairs, right sides facing, leaving small openings to turn through. Turn right side out, close openings and topstitch around flap edges. Place pockets with folds of flaps to seamline, topstitch in position. Turn up hems of skirt and sleeves and slip stitch in place. Sew buttons to left front and to trim pockets.

SELVAGE

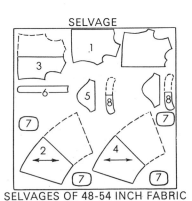

SELVAGES OF 48-54 INCH FABRIC

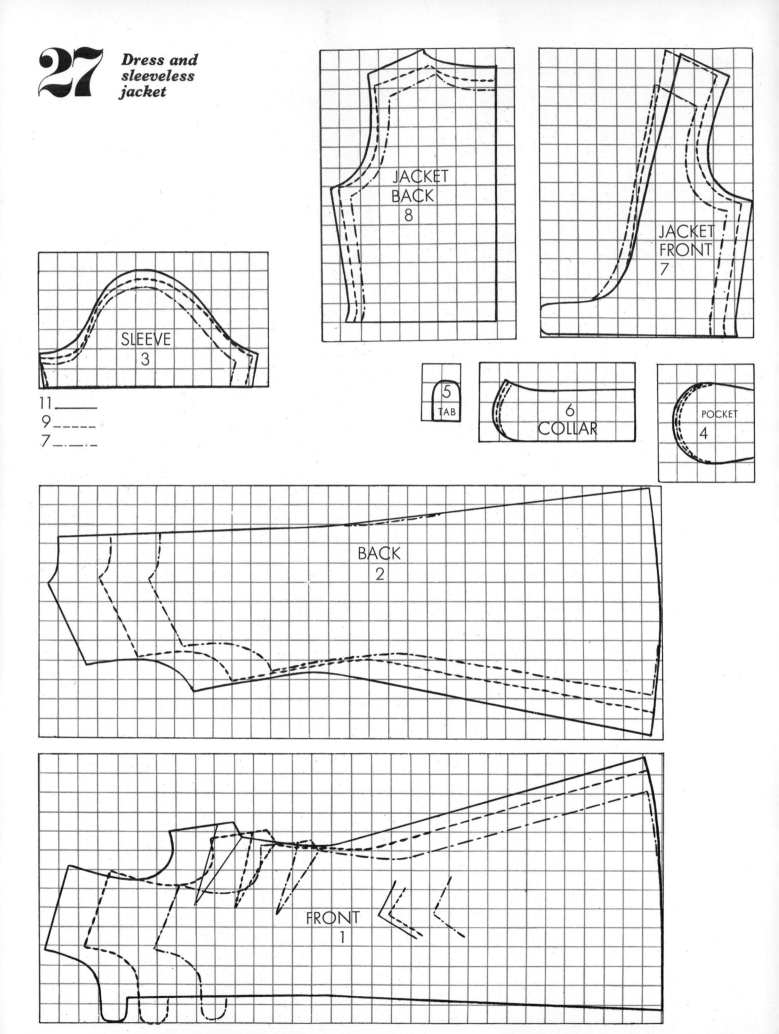

27 *Dress and sleeveless jacket*

JACKET BACK 8

JACKET FRONT 7

SLEEVE 3

11 ———
9 – – – –
7 –·–·–·

5 TAB

6 COLLAR

POCKET 4

BACK 2

FRONT 1

28

Front-buttoned dress with dropped waist

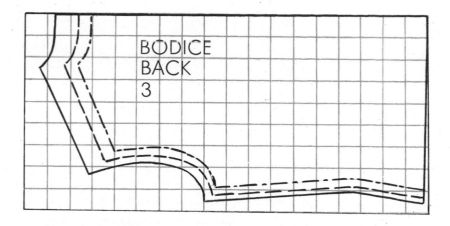

BODICE
BACK
3

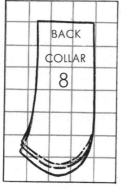

BACK
COLLAR
8

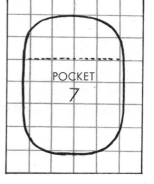

POCKET
7

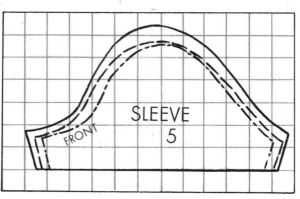

FRONT

SLEEVE
5

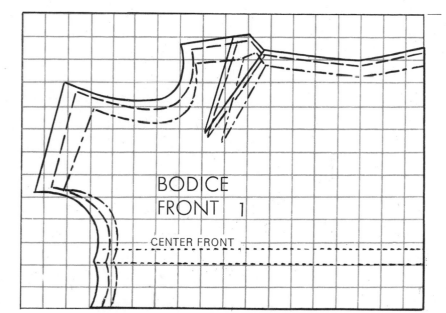

BODICE
FRONT 1

CENTER FRONT

12 ——————
10 – – – – –
8 –·–·–·–

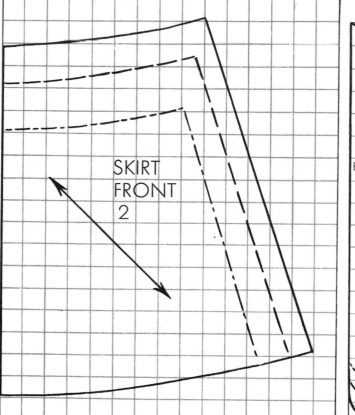

SKIRT
FRONT
2

BAND
6

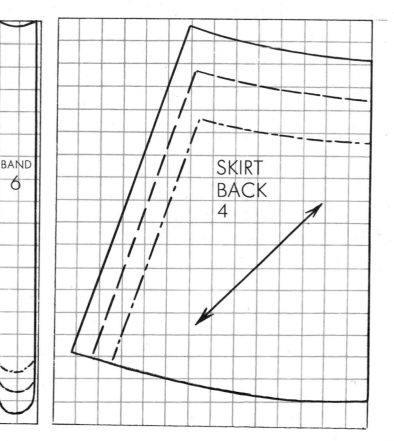

SKIRT
BACK
4

29

Girl's coat and boy's duffle coat with hood, both fully reversible, and adaptations of the same pattern. Bath robe also adapted from the same pattern

30

Long, snug quilted house coat and collarless, zip-front coat, both adaptations of the same basic pattern

Bath robe

Fabric required

Sizes	9	11	13	yrs
Bath robe (Version A)				
36 inch fabric	$2\frac{1}{2}$	$2\frac{5}{8}$	3	yds
Piping cord	$3\frac{1}{2}$	$3\frac{1}{2}$	$3\frac{1}{2}$	yds

To make pattern

See Know-how, also for patterns for neck facings if required.

To cut out

See Know-how. Omit neck facings in terry cloth. *Remember to add turnings and hem allowances.*

Making the bath robe
Version A

Stitch shoulder, side and sleeve seams. Press. Stitch collar band at top edge, turn to right side and press. Pin collar to neck edge at center front, fold front facing to right side over collar, attach collar with bias strip (see Working Details) if using terry, otherwise join seams of neck facings, pin to neck edge over collar and front facing. Stitch along neck seam, turn to right side and press. Make three vertical buttonholes in left front (see Working Details). Stitch sleeves into armholes. Seam falls toward back, so fold sleeve until it forms "normal" sleeve shape (see Working Details). Turn up and slip stitch sleeve and lower hems. Starting at right front, sew cord around neck edge at base of collar and down left front, making loops between buttonholes as pictured. Turn in $1\frac{1}{2}$ inches at tops of pockets. Trim pockets and sleeves similarly with cord. Slip stitch pockets in place. Sew buttons on right front. *Remember—each square equals one inch square.*

Girl's coat and duffle coat

Fabric required

Sizes	9	11	13	yrs
Girl's coat (Version B)				
Boy's duffle (Version C)				
54 inch fabric	$1\frac{3}{4}$	$1\frac{7}{8}$	2	yds
Buttons				
Version B 2 large covered				
Version C 11 round leather, 11 flat				

To make pattern

Version B. Use diagram for Version A, adding $2\frac{1}{2}$ inches to coat length for all sizes. Version C. Use diagram for Version A but follow dotted line at center front marked Duffle Coat.

To cut out

Cut off selvages before cutting out reversible fabric. Allow $\frac{3}{4}$ inch on main seams. Version B, allow $1\frac{1}{4}$ inches at neck, $1\frac{1}{2}$ inches at sleeve hem, $\frac{3}{8}$ inch on pockets, omit seam allowance on front edges. For neck band cut strip 3 inches by 30 inches. Version C, allow $\frac{3}{8}$ inch at front edges and hems, $\frac{1}{4}$ inch on tabs. Omit turnings on hood facings.

Making the coats
Version B

See Know-how for sewing reversible fabrics. Stitch shoulders, sides and sleeves with flat fell seams. Stitch sleeves into armholes (see Version A) making strap seams. Stitch edges on fronts and pockets (see method for edges in Working Details). Baste neck band edges similarly. Fold band in half, plain side out and fit around neck with neck edge fitting well up into fold. Slip stitch onto tweed side. Make bias-cut loops from single plain fabric

for buttons. Stitch one loop into each end of strip. Stitch strip onto plain side. To finish coat and sleeve hems, trim away tweed layer $\frac{3}{8}$ inch, turn under plain side and slip stitch onto tweed. Sew one button on each side, reinforcing with small square of single fabric. Position pockets, one on tweed side, one on plain and slip stitch in place.

Version C

Stitch shoulder, side and sleeve seams and insert sleeves as Version B. Join curved head seams of hood with flat fell seam. Fold facings onto tweed side and hem, or cut off along fold line and make neat, using method for edges as in Version B. Join hood to neck edge of coat, tweed sides together, nick inner curved edge and flat fell seam, leaving about 1 inch unsewn at each end. Clip neck

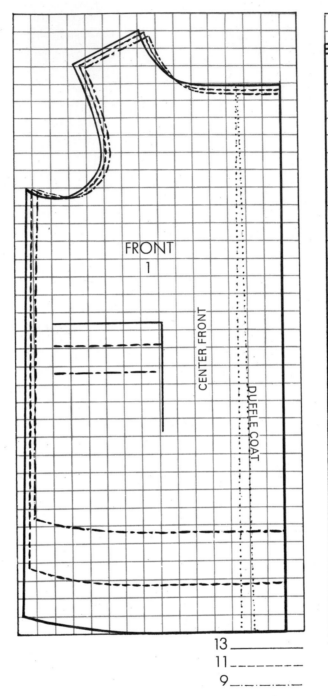
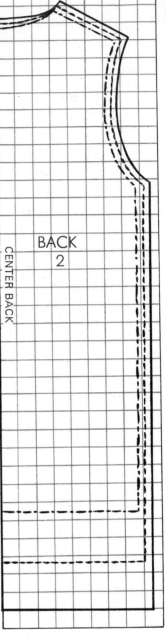

FRONT 1

CENTER FRONT

DUFFLE COAT

BACK 2

CENTER BACK

13 ⎯⎯⎯⎯
11 ⎯ ⎯ ⎯ ⎯
9 ⎯ · ⎯ · ⎯

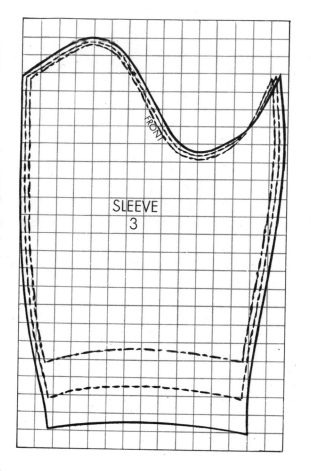

SLEEVE
3

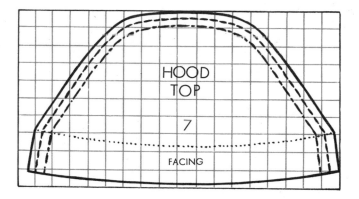

HOOD
TOP
7
FACING

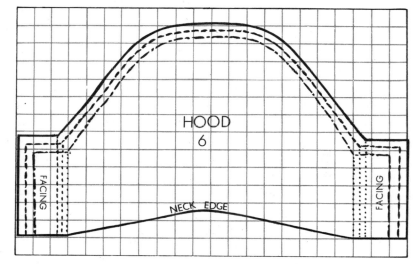

HOOD
6

FACING

NECK EDGE

FACING

COLLAR 8

POCKET
4

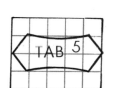

TAB 5

edge to point where hood joins neck seam. Trim seam allowance to ⅜ inch. Make neat neck edge, front edge, pockets, tabs, lower and sleeve hems, using method for edges as in Version B. (Rip seams a little and turn in each part separately at hems. Then join up seams again). Make buttonholes horizontally at each end of tabs (see Working Details). Fold coat fronts over, left over right for 2¼ inches. Position four tabs down front to mark button placings. Sew leather buttons on tweed, flat buttons on plain side, sewing through both so that they do not pull too much on fabric. Position tab at base of hood and sew on buttons, sew two buttons at left side of hood to fix tab when not in use. Sew on pockets as Version B.

Remember—each square equals one inch square.

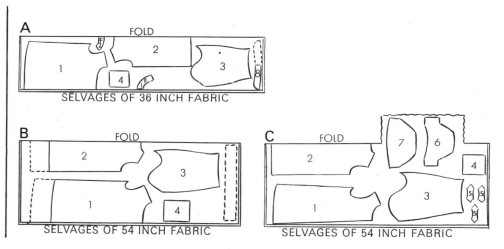

A FOLD

SELVAGES OF 36 INCH FABRIC

B FOLD

SELVAGES OF 54 INCH FABRIC

C FOLD

SELVAGES OF 54 INCH FABRIC

30

Coat and long house coat

Fabric required

Sizes	5	7	9	yrs
Coat				
(Version A)				
36 inch fabric	$2\frac{1}{4}$	$2\frac{3}{8}$	$2\frac{5}{8}$	yds
48 inch fabric	$1\frac{5}{8}$	$1\frac{3}{4}$	2	yds
Zipper	22	24	26	ins
(open end)				
Braid	4	4	$4\frac{1}{2}$	yds
Dressing gown				
(Version B)				
36 inch quilted				
fabric	$3\frac{1}{8}$	$3\frac{1}{4}$	$3\frac{1}{2}$	yds
36 inch contrast	$\frac{3}{8}$	$\frac{3}{8}$	$\frac{3}{8}$	yd
Cord for				
trimming	$2\frac{1}{2}$	$2\frac{1}{2}$	$2\frac{1}{2}$	yds

To make pattern

See Know-how, also to make pattern for back neck facing. Version B, extend pattern to full length, also make pattern for front neck facing, continuing down to hem. Omit sleeve bands on quilted fabric.

To cut out

See Know-how. *Remember to add turnings* to all pattern pieces except bound edges. Version B, see Working Details, working with quilting. Add 2 inch hem allowance. For frills, cut four strips of contrast, $3\frac{1}{4}$ inches by 36 inches.

Making the coats

Version A

Stitch front darts, shoulder, side and sleeve seams. Press. Stitch sleeves into armholes (see Working Details). Join back facing to front at shoulders. With wrong sides together, baste facings to neck edge down front and around curve at lower edge. Insert open ended zipper into center front opening (see Working Details) stitch near edge of zipper tape to leave room for edge to be bound afterward. Stitch braid around neck, front and hem edges. Stitch braid to tops of sleeve bands. Stitch seams of bands. Sew bands to sleeves, right sides of bands to wrong sides of sleeves. Fold bands up over turnings to right side. Fold pockets in half, right sides together and stitch around curved edges, leaving space to turn through to right side. Close opening and press. Trim pockets with braid and slip stitch in place.

Version B

Stitch front darts, shoulder, side and sleeve seams and insert sleeves as Version A. Join three frill pieces into one length. Fold in half, wrong sides facing and press. Gather raw edges to fit right front and neck edge as far as left front. Stitch to edge of house coat. Hem sleeves. Cut fourth frill piece in half, join ends into two circles and stitch to sleeves similarly. Stitch neck and front facings (see Working Details). Turn up hem. Stitch cord above frills. Sew on snap fasteners.

Remember—each square equals one inch square.

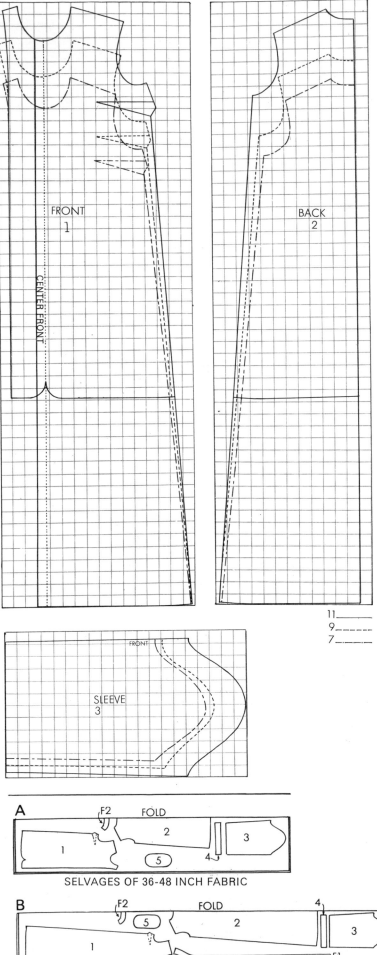

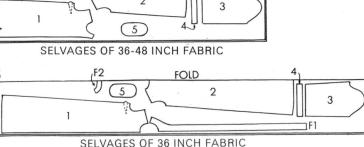

A
SELVAGES OF 36-48 INCH FABRIC

B
SELVAGES OF 36 INCH FABRIC

31

Warm chevron-striped poncho decorated with deep fringe

Fabric required

Sizes	5	10	yrs
54 inch fabric	1	1	yd
Fringe (optional)	3¼	3½	yds

N.B. If striped fabric is used it should have a clearly definable warp and weft which is the same on both sides of the fabric.

To cut out

Trim top edge of fabric along the grain. Measure 27 inches along this line, from selvage, for Size 5 years, 30½ inches for Size 10 years, fold over exactly on the diagonal and cut along the diagonal line. Move the triangle point A along the fabric to match the stripes on the diagonal (diagram 1) so that when stitched and opened out the stripes form chevrons down the center of the square. Cut out this second triangle.

Making the poncho

Stitch both triangles together along the diagonal line to make a 26½ inch square for Size 5 years, 30 inch square for Size 10 years. Press. To make neck opening, fold square, matching center seam, so that one point of center is 2½ inches lower than the other (diagram 2). This is for the back. Now fold in half again along seamline (diagram 3). Measure around head (as for a hat) and divide by four. Find this quarter measurement with tape measure by moving it down from the point. Pin a line across, shaping it into a slight curve (diagram 3). Cut off fabric close to pin line. Open out poncho. For padded neck roll, cut bias strip, 2½ inches wide by neck hole measurement (allow for bias join). Join to form circle. Fold strip in half and with raw edges to neck edge, stitch strip around neck opening, right side out. Leave small opening to allow for padding insertion. Press. Thread several thicknesses of knitting worsted through bias strip to make a nice thick roll. Close opening. To make fringe, cut four strips along straight grain, 2½ inches by 27 inches for Size 5, or 2½ inches by 30 inches for Size 10. Be sure all strips are cut from same grain of fabric. Turn under edges of square and top stitch each side flat on to a strip. Unravel the long threads from each strip to form fringe. Or trim with ready-made fringe. Crochet or buy braid to trim edge of poncho. Add tassels if desired.

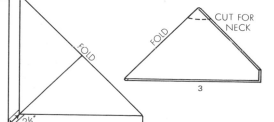

32

Gaily trimmed pinafore

Fabric required

Sizes	3	5	7	yrs
36 inch fabric (with nap)	$1\frac{1}{2}$	$1\frac{1}{2}$	$1\frac{5}{8}$	yds
Straight seam binding	$5\frac{1}{2}$	$5\frac{3}{4}$	6	yds

To make pattern

See Know-how.

To cut out

See Know-how and follow the cutting layout. Place frill 4 twice to fold. Remember the pattern has no hem or seam allowances so add these when cutting out. No hem allowance needed at lower edge of front, back and gusset. No seam allowances needed at neck edge of front and back, top edge of gusset and straight edges and ends of frilled sleeve.

Making up

Turn in seam allowance at center back and slip stitch or machine in place. Make French seams at shoulders (see Working Details). For each sleeve cut a piece of binding the length of frill and fold in half lengthways. Baste and top stitch to right side of frill, 1 inch from straight edge (optional). To bind outer (straight) edges of frill press binding in half and slip raw edge well in to fold. Baste in place, mitering corners. Stitch through all three thicknesses along inner edges of binding. Bind top edge of gusset as for frill. Turn in seam allowance on all edges of pocket and baste. Topstitch top edge $\frac{1}{4}$ inch from fold. Place pocket in center of left gusset, $\frac{1}{2}$ inch from hem line. Topstitch in position $\frac{1}{4}$ inch from sides and lower edge. Gather top edge of frill between marks and with right sides together stitch into armhole. Neaten seam. With right sides together stitch gusset to front and back. Trim seam, press and make French seam on right side of fabric, stitching $\frac{1}{4}$ inch from first seam. Bind hem of pinafore as for frill, flattening French seams at hem (towards gussets). Bind the neck edge. At back opening attach 9 inch lengths of binding for ties, one at the neck edge, one 7 inches below. On right side attach the ties at edge of opening, on left side attach ties $\frac{3}{4}$ inch in from edge. (Alternatively fasten back with five buttons and buttonholes.)

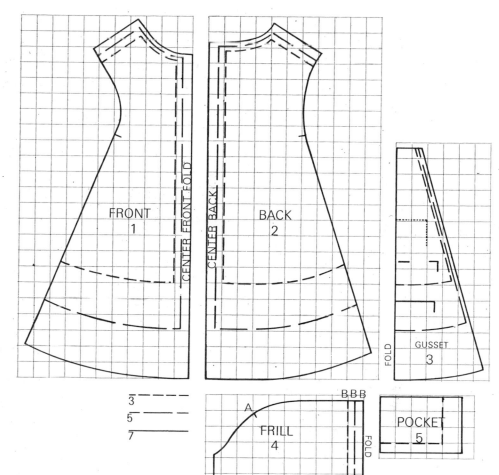

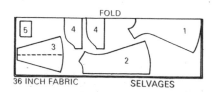

33

Very simple jumper dress with buttoned shoulders. Designed for jersey

Fabric required

Sizes	3	5	7	yrs
60 inch fabric	1	1⅛	1¼	yds
Buttons	2	2	2	

Contrasting thread for topstitching

To make pattern

See Know-how. Make front neck and front armhole facing in one, back neck and back armhole facing in one.

To cut out

See Know-how and follow the cutting layouts. Cut pocket piece 3 twice on double fabric. Remember the pattern has no hem or seam allowances so add these when cutting out.

Making up

(Where topstitching is mentioned a machine satin stitch can be substituted.) Stitch side seams of dress and facings. Place facings to dress, right sides together, and stitch in one continuous seam round front, armholes and back. Clip seam allowances and turn right side out. Press seam. Topstitch ⅝ inch from neck and armhole edges in contrasting thread. Turn up hem and slip stitch in place. Topstitch 1¾ inches from hem line. With right sides together, stitch pocket sections in pairs, leaving small opening at lower edge to turn through. Turn right side out, slip stitch openings to close, press and topstitch ¼ inch from top edges. Topstitch ⅝ inch from remaining edges and slip stitch in position on dress front. Make vertical buttonhole on each back shoulder strap, front end of buttonhole ¾ inch from pointed end of shoulder strap. Sew buttons on front shoulder straps, 1 inch in from end of strap.

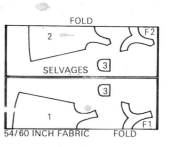

54/60 INCH FABRIC

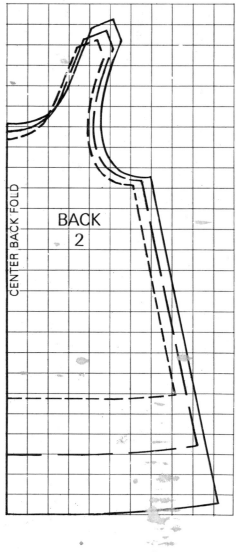

FRONT 1

CENTER FRONT FOLD

CENTER BACK FOLD

BACK 2

3	
5	
7	

3

POCKET

34

Short-sleeved dress with contrasting curved yoke. Designed for jersey

Fabric required

Sizes	2	4	6	yrs
60 inch patterned fabric	$\frac{5}{8}$	$\frac{3}{4}$	$\frac{3}{4}$	yd
60 inch plain fabric	$\frac{3}{8}$	$\frac{3}{8}$	$\frac{3}{8}$	yd
Zipper	9	9	9	ins
Hooks and eyes				

To make pattern

See Know-how.

To cut out

See Know-how and follow the cutting layouts. Cut collar 5 and pocket 7 twice on double fabric. Remember the pattern has no hem or seam allowances so add these when cutting out.

Making up

(All topstitching $\frac{1}{4}$ inch from edge or seam line.)

Stitch dart at back shoulder. Gather top edge of front for 4 inches either side of center front. Stitch front to yoke adjusting fullness to fit. Press turnings towards yoke and topstitch. Stitch side and shoulder seams. Press. Make up collars into two separate pieces and attach to neck edge (see Working Details) with rounded ends to center front. Topstitch edges of collars. Stitch center back seam from lower edge to within $9\frac{1}{2}$ inches of neck edge. Press. Insert zipper into back opening (see Working Details). Stitch sleeve seam. Working on each sleeve band, stitch short ends together to form circles. Stitch lower edge of sleeve band to lower edge of sleeve, right side of band to wrong side of sleeve. Press seam allowance towards sleeve. Turn band to right side of sleeve, turn in seam allowance on remaining edge and topstitch to sleeve. Topstitch lower edge of band. Stitch sleeve into armhole (see Working Details). With right sides together stitch pocket sections in pairs, leaving small opening at lower edge to turn through. Turn right side out, slip stitch openings to close. Press. Topstitch top edge. Topstitch pockets in place to dress front. Fasten back edges of collar with hooks and eyes. Turn up hem and slip stitch or hem invisibly in place.

 35

Buttoned dress with contrasting yoke, sleeve bands and patch pockets. Designed for jersey

Fabric required

Sizes	4	6	8	yrs
60 inch patterned fabric	$\frac{7}{8}$	1	1	yd
60 inch plain fabric	$\frac{3}{8}$	$\frac{3}{8}$	$\frac{3}{8}$	yd
Buttons	5	5	5	

To make pattern

See Know-how.

To cut out

See Know-how and follow the cutting layouts. Cut collar 5 and pocket 8 twice on double fabric. Remember the pattern has no hem or seam allowances so add these when cutting out.

Making up

(All topstitching $\frac{1}{4}$ inch from seam lines or folded edges.)

Stitch darts in back yoke. Stitch yokes to back and fronts. Press turnings towards yokes and topstitch. Stitch shoulder seams. Stitch front band facings to fronts, right sides together. Press turnings towards band. Fold band $1\frac{1}{8}$ inches from seam line and turn to outside. Stitch across top of band from fold to seam line. Turn right side out and press. Make up collar and attach to neck edge (see Working Details). Topstitch edge of collar. Stitch sleeve seams. Working on each sleeve, stitch shorter edges of cuff together to make circle. Press. Stitch straight edge of cuff to lower edge of sleeve, right side of band to wrong side of sleeve. Press seam allowance towards sleeve. Turn cuff to right side of sleeve, turn in seam allowance on remaining edge and topstitch in place to right side of sleeve. Stitch sleeve into armhole (see Working Details). With right sides together, stitch pocket sections in pairs, leaving small opening at lower edge to turn through. Turn right side out, slip stitch openings to close. Press. Topstitch $1\frac{3}{8}$ inch from top edge. Topstitch in place to fronts $\frac{1}{4}$ inch from other edges. Turn up hem and sew in place. Topstitch front band and hem line. Make five evenly spaced vertical buttonholes centrally on right front band. Attach corresponding buttons.

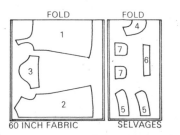

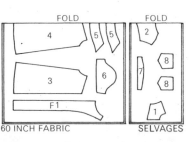

34

*Short-sleeved dress with
contrasting curved yoke.
Designed for jersey*

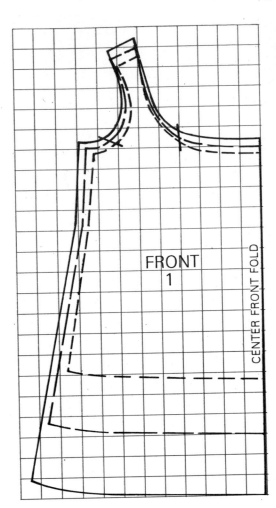

FRONT
1

CENTER FRONT FOLD

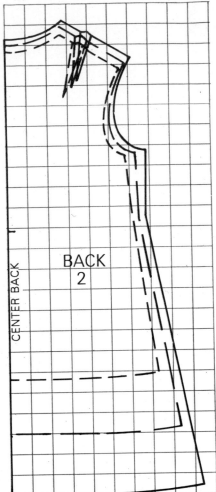

BACK
2

CENTER BACK

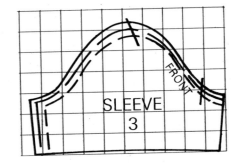

SLEEVE
3

FRONT

FRONT
YOKE
4

CENTER FRONT FOLD

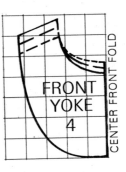

CENTER BACK

COLLAR 5

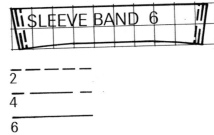

SLEEVE BAND 6

2
4
6

POCKET
7

35

Buttoned dress
with contrasting yoke,
sleeve bands
and patch pockets.
Designed for jersey

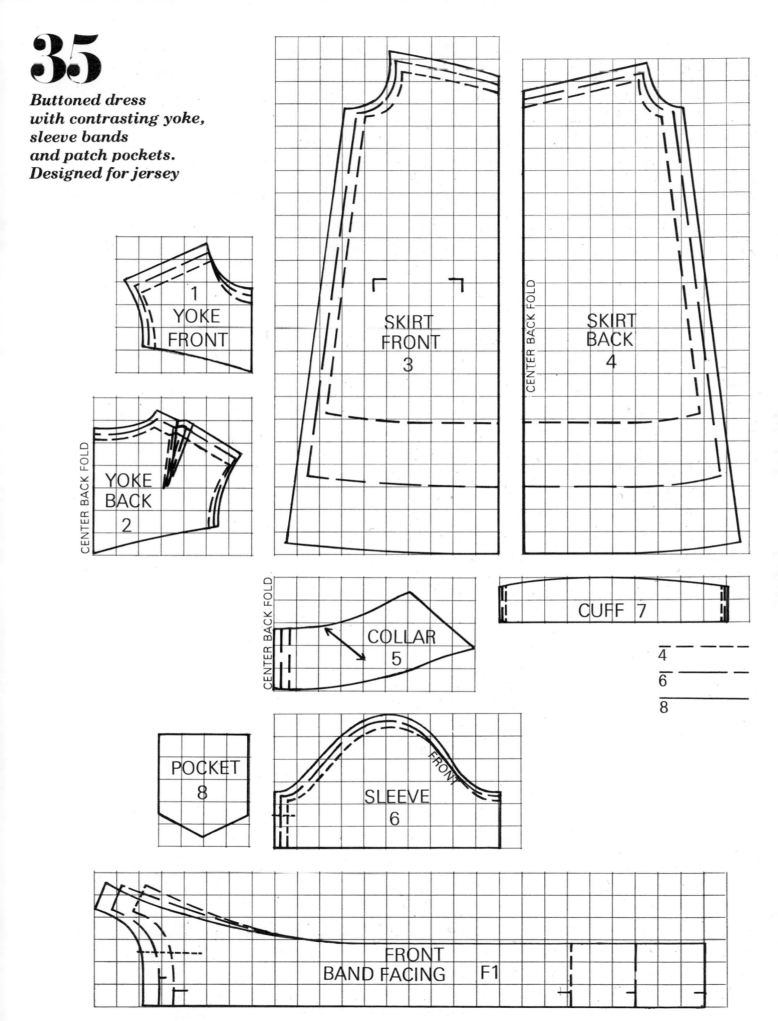

1
YOKE
FRONT

YOKE
BACK
2
CENTER BACK FOLD

SKIRT
FRONT
3

SKIRT
BACK
4
CENTER BACK FOLD

COLLAR
5
CENTER BACK FOLD

CUFF 7

4
6
8

POCKET
8

SLEEVE
6
FRONT

FRONT
BAND FACING   F1

36

Simple dress with cap sleeves and contrasting yoke. Designed for jersey

Fabric required

Sizes	8	10	12	yrs
60 inch patterned fabric	$\frac{7}{8}$	1	1	yd
60 inch plain fabric	$\frac{3}{8}$	$\frac{3}{8}$	$\frac{3}{8}$	yd
Interfacing	$\frac{1}{8}$	$\frac{1}{8}$	$\frac{1}{8}$	yd
Zipper	12	14	14	ins

To make pattern

See Know-how, also for patterns for neck facing.

To cut out

See Know-how and follow the cutting layouts. Place cap sleeve 5 to fold four times. Cut cap sleeve to fold of interfacing twice. Remember the pattern has no hem or seam allowances so add these when cutting out.

Making up

Stitch darts in yoke backs. Press. Stitch front yoke to front, back yokes to backs. Press. Stitch side and shoulder seams. Press. Stitch center back seam from lower edge to within $12\frac{1}{2}$ inches of neck edge for size 8 and $14\frac{1}{2}$ inches for sizes 10 and 12 years. Insert zipper into back opening (see Working Details). Stitch neck facings (see Working Details). Baste interfacing to wrong side of two cap sleeves and use these as upper caps. With right sides together stitch shoulder cap sections in pairs around longer, curved edges. Turn right side out and press. With right sides together, place cap sleeves to armholes, pointed ends meeting at underarm seam. Stitch top, interfaced, layer in place. Press seam towards cap. Turn in remaining edge and slip stitch to seam line. Turn up hem and slip stitch in place.

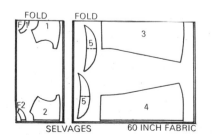

Classic topstitched
V-necked jumper dress.
Designed for jersey

Fabric required

Sizes	10	12	14	yrs
60 inch fabric	1	$1\frac{1}{4}$	$1\frac{1}{2}$	yds
Zipper	14	16	16	ins

To make pattern

See Know-how, also for neck and armhole facings. Pleat back neck dart closed before tracing off back neck facing.

To cut out

See Know-how and follow the cutting layouts. Remember the pattern has no hem or seam allowances so add these when cutting out.

Making up

Stitch darts in bodice back and front. Press. Stitch side and shoulder seams of bodice, side seams of skirt. Press. Stitch neck and armhole facings (see Working Details). Stitch bodice to skirt, matching seams. Press. Stitch center back seam from lower edge to within $14\frac{1}{2}$ inches of neck edge for size 10 and $16\frac{1}{2}$ inches for sizes 12 and 14 years. Insert zipper in center back opening (see Working Details). Turn up hem and sew in place. Topstitch $\frac{1}{2}$ inch from neck and armhole edges and hem line.

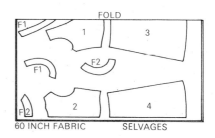

36

Simple dress with cap sleeves and contrasting yoke. Designed for jersey

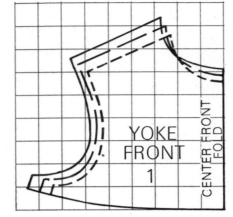

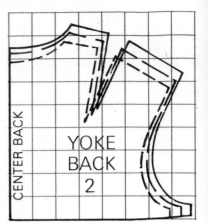

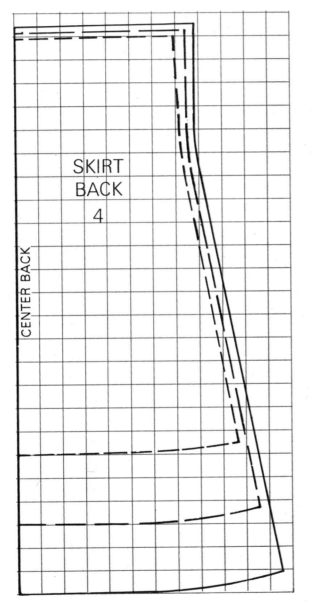

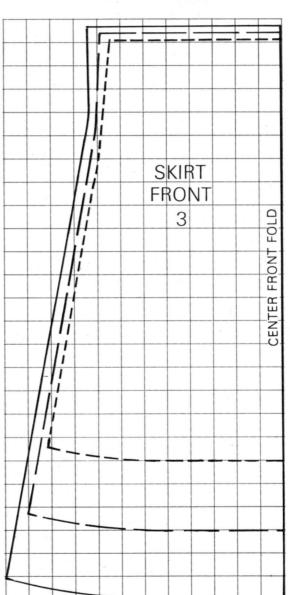

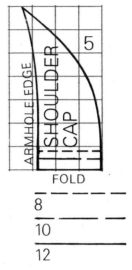

37

**Classic topstitched
V-necked jumper dress.
Designed for jersey**

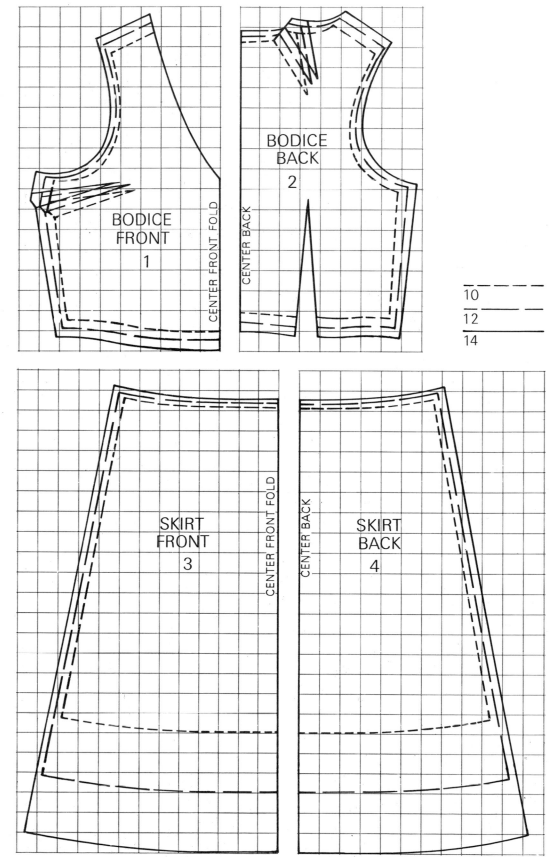

BODICE
FRONT
1

CENTER FRONT FOLD

BODICE
BACK
2

CENTER BACK

10
12
14

SKIRT
FRONT
3

CENTER FRONT FOLD

CENTER BACK

SKIRT
BACK
4

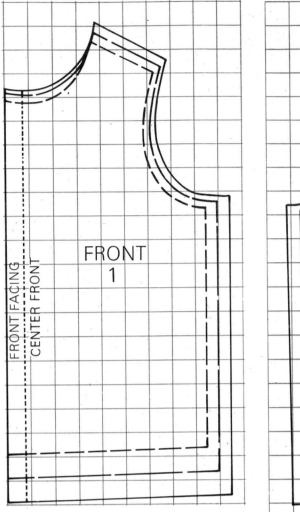

FRONT
1

FRONT FACING
CENTER FRONT

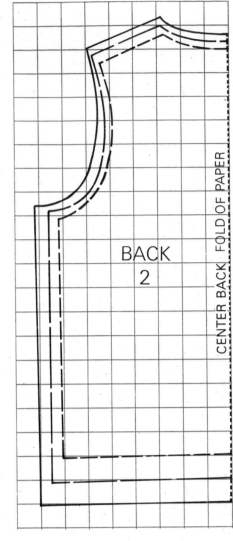

BACK
2

CENTER BACK   FOLD OF PAPER

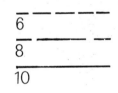

6	- - - - -
8	- · - · -
10	————

38

Fringed leather jerkin

Fabric required

Sizes   6   8   10 yrs

Take all pattern pieces to a leather shop and lay them out on the skins to see how many you require, this will depend on the size of the skins.

To make pattern

See Know-how.

To cut out

See Know-how and special remarks on leather below. No hem allowance needed. Remember to add turnings $\frac{3}{8}$ inch wide. Cut thong $\frac{1}{4}$ inch wide 52 inches long, piecing where necessary to make length.

Making up

Stitch side and shoulder seam. Fold front facing to inside and glue in place. Clip neck and armhole seam allowances and turn to inside. Glue into place. Topstitch $\frac{1}{4}$ inch from all finished edges for extra strength. Punch 4 eyelets in each front, $2\frac{1}{2}$ inches apart, $\frac{1}{2}$ inch in from front edge, top one $1\frac{5}{8}$ inches from neck edge. Cut fringe in lower edge, $3\frac{1}{2}$ inches long $\frac{1}{4}$ inch wide. Thread thong through eyelet holes.

Working with leather

Make sure pattern is the correct size, if necessary making it up in a cheap cotton first to ensure a perfect fit, as stitch marks will show if leather is altered. Place pattern on wrong side of skin and hold in place with weights or transparent adhesive tape; pins would leave marks. Cut only one layer at a time, remembering to reverse pattern for left and right sides. Although leather skins have no grain of thread try to keep center front and back of pattern parallel to backbone mark of skin. Try to avoid thin pieces of skin.

Marking pattern detail. Use tailor's chalk on wrong side of skin.

Stitching. Use leather needle on machine or when hand stitching. Hold edges together with staples within the seam allowance or paper clips.

Seams. Thinner skins can be stitched normally and pressed with a warm iron over brown paper. Glue seam allowances back. Glue up hems. For thicker skins place one layer over other, matching seam lines, and stitch flat with two rows of stitches.

After care. Some skins are washable but if you choose a non-washable skin have it professionally cleaned.

39

Simply shaped polka dot dress with contrast bands

Fabric required

Sizes	5	7	9	yrs
36 inch fabric and	$1\frac{1}{2}$	$1\frac{3}{4}$	$1\frac{3}{4}$	yds
36 inch contrast fabric	$\frac{1}{4}$	$\frac{1}{4}$	$\frac{1}{4}$	yd
or				
45 inch fabric and	$1\frac{3}{8}$	$1\frac{1}{2}$	$1\frac{1}{2}$	yds
45 inch contrast fabric	$\frac{1}{4}$	$\frac{1}{4}$	$\frac{1}{4}$	yd
Zipper	12	12	14	ins

To make pattern

See Know-how.

To cut out

See Know-how and follow cutting layouts. Remember the pattern has no hem or seam allowances so add these when cutting out. Add $\frac{3}{8}$ inch turning to inner edge of facings.

Making up

Stitch shoulder, side and center front seams. Press. Stitch center back seam from lower edge to within $12\frac{1}{2}$ inches of neck edge for sizes 5 and 7 and $14\frac{1}{2}$ inches for size 9 years. Press. Insert zipper into back opening (see Working Details). Place neck facing to inside of neck line, right side of facing meeting wrong side of dress. Stitch. Press, trim and clip seam. Turn facing to outside and baste round neck seam. Turn in $\frac{3}{8}$ inch along inside edge of facing and slip stitch in place. Stitch seam of armhole facings. Press. Place to armhole edges, right side of facing to wrong side of dress. Stitch. Press, trim and clip seam. Turn outside as for neck facing. Slip stitch in place. Turn up hem of dress and sew in place.

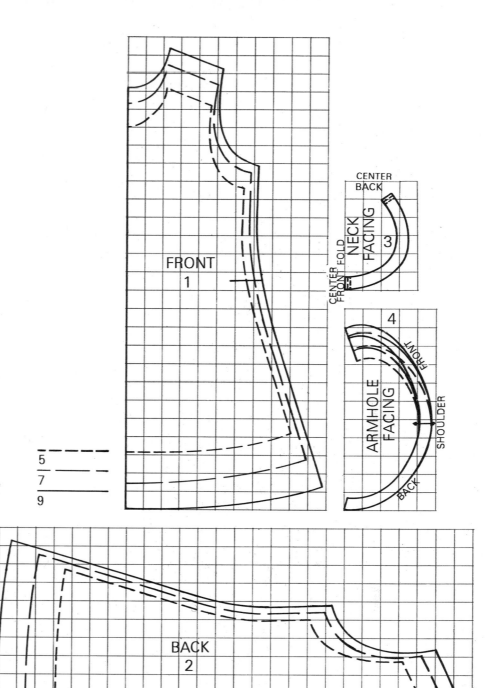

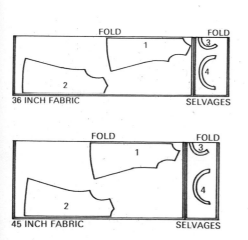

36 INCH FABRIC

45 INCH FABRIC

40

Gay checked dress with a pleated skirt

Fabric required

Sizes	6	8	10	yrs
36 inch fabric	$1\frac{3}{4}$	$1\frac{7}{8}$	2	yds
36 inch lining	$\frac{1}{4}$	$\frac{1}{4}$	$\frac{1}{4}$	yd
Buttons	6	6	6	

To make pattern

See Know-how.

To cut out

See Know-how and follow the cutting layout. Place collar 6 twice to fold. Cut pocket 2 and sleeve 7 in lining (on straight grain of fabric). Remember the pattern has no hem or seam allowances so add these when cutting out, adding 2 inch hem only for skirt.

Making up

Stitch darts, side and shoulder seams of bodice, easing back shoulder slightly to fit front. Stitch side seams of skirt. Press. Turn up skirt hem and slip stitch in place. Pleat skirt, placing line onto adjacent arrows (see Working Details), baste pleats in place. Stitch bodice to skirt, matching seams. Press turnings towards bodice. Fold front facings to outside and stitch along neck edge for $\frac{1}{2}$ inch. Trim and snip seam allowance at end of stitching. Turn right side out and baste remaining neck edges of facing to neck edge of bodice. Make collar and attach to raw neck edge (see Working Details). Baste sleeve lining to sleeve and treat as one layer. Stitch sleeve seam. Press. Stitch sleeve into armhole (see Working Details). Turn up sleeve hem and slip stitch in place. Place pocket section to lining section, right sides facing, and stitch together, leaving small opening at lower edge to turn through. Turn right side out and slip stitch opening to close. Press and topstitch $\frac{1}{2}$ inch from top edge. Slip stitch in place to left front. Make 6 evenly spaced buttonholes by hand or machine (4 on bodice, 2 on skirt) on right front, the top one $\frac{5}{8}$ inch from neck line. Sew on corresponding buttons.

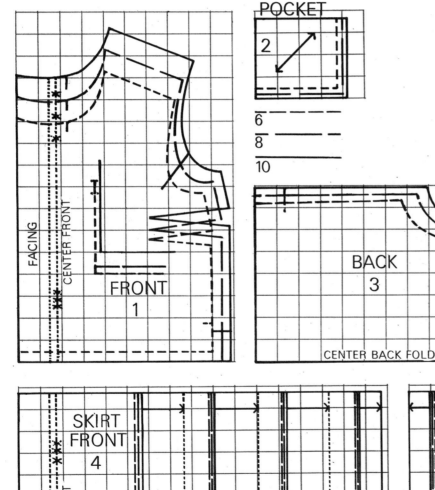

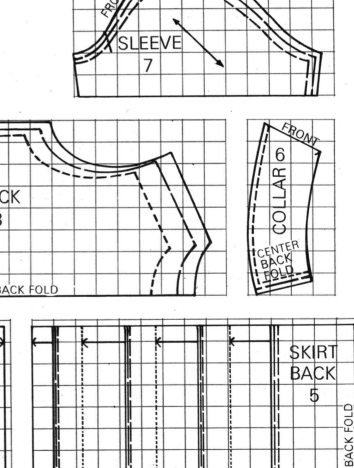

41

A summer outfit, gathered skirt with brief V-necked top. Skirt has side opening

Fabric required

Sizes	5	7	9	yrs
36 inch fabric	$1\frac{1}{2}$	$1\frac{1}{2}$	$1\frac{5}{8}$	yds
Buttons	6	6	6	
Hooks and eyes	2	2	2	

To make pattern

See Know-how, also for armhole and neck and front facings.

To cut out

See Know-how and follow the cutting lay-outs. Remember the pattern has no hem or seam allowances so add these when cutting out.

Making up

Top: Stitch darts. Press. Stitch side and shoulder seams. Press. Stitch neck and arm-hole facings (see Working Details). Turn up hem and slip stitch in place. Make 3 evenly spaced buttonholes in right front $\frac{5}{8}$ inch in from front edge, the top one where marked. Sew on corresponding buttons.

Skirt: To neaten opening on left hand side of skirt place skirt back facing to skirt back, right sides together. Stitch and turn right side out. Press. To neaten the left front turn facing to inside along fold line and press. Slip stitch both facings in place. Trim $1\frac{1}{2}$ inch along the right side seam edge of both back and front. Stitch front and back of skirt together at right hand side seam, right sides together. Trim $1\frac{1}{2}$ inch from one end of waist band. Fold lengthways and stitch across ends. Gather top edge of skirt to fit waist band, adjusting fullness evenly. Stitch one layer of waist band to waist edge of skirt. Turn waist band to inside and slip stitch in place. Fasten waist band with hooks and eyes. Make 3 buttonholes in skirt front where marked. Sew on corresponding buttons. Turn up hem of skirt and sew in place.

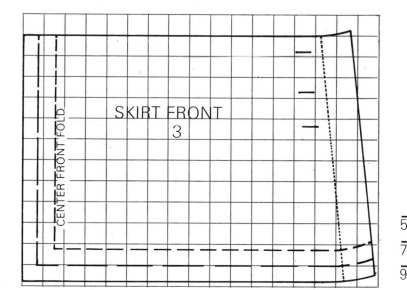

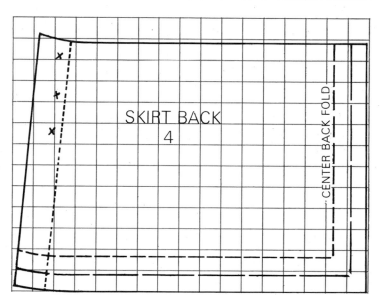

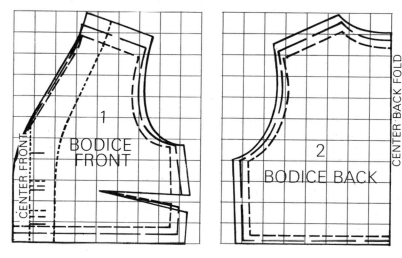

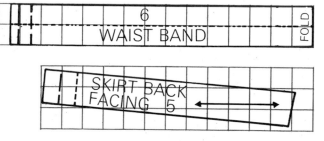

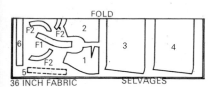

42

Simple crisp blazer for girls

Fabric required

Sizes	8	10	12	yrs
45 inch fabric				
or				
54 inch fabric	$1\frac{1}{4}$	$1\frac{3}{8}$	$1\frac{3}{8}$	yds
36 inch lining	$1\frac{7}{8}$	2	2	yds
Interfacing	$\frac{5}{8}$	$\frac{5}{8}$	$\frac{5}{8}$	yd
Buttons	3	3	3	

To make pattern

See Know-how, also for back neck facing pattern. Close dart in back neck before tracing off back neck facing. Pockets same size for sizes 8 and 10 years.

To cut out

See Know-how and follow cutting layouts. Remember the pattern has no hem or seam allowances so add these when cutting out. Cut two lower pocket pieces 4, one upper pocket piece 5 from blazer fabric and again in lining fabric. Cut lining as jacket omitting facings and pockets. Cut interfacing for fronts and back neck (see Working Details).

Making up

Stitch darts in fronts, back and sleeves. Press. Baste interfacing to wrong side of front edge and back neck edge (see Working Details). Stitch side, shoulder and sleeve seams. Press. Stitch facings (see Working Details). Stitch sleeves into armholes. Press. Turn up hems and slip stitch in place. Topstitch $\frac{1}{2}$ inch from neck and front edges and hem line. Arrange fabric and lining pocket sections in pairs. Stitch, with right sides together, leaving small opening to turn through. Turn right side out, close openings and press. Topstitch all edges of lower pockets and side and lower edges of top pocket $\frac{1}{2}$ inch from edges. Slip stitch pockets to jacket fronts. Make up and insert lining (see Working Details). Make three horizontal buttonholes down center front of right front. Sew on buttons to correspond.

43

Boy's blazer

Fabric required

Sizes	6	8	10	yrs
45 inch fabric				
or				
54 inch fabric	$1\frac{1}{4}$	$1\frac{1}{4}$	$1\frac{3}{8}$	yds
36 inch lining	$1\frac{7}{8}$	$1\frac{7}{8}$	2	yds
Interfacing	$\frac{1}{2}$	$\frac{5}{8}$	$\frac{5}{8}$	yd
Buttons	3	3	3	

To make pattern

See Know-how, also for back neck facing pattern. Pocket same size for sizes 6 and 8 years.

To cut out

See Know-how and instructions and cutting layouts for girl's blazer.

Making up

As for girl's blazer, reversing buttons and buttonholes.

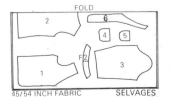

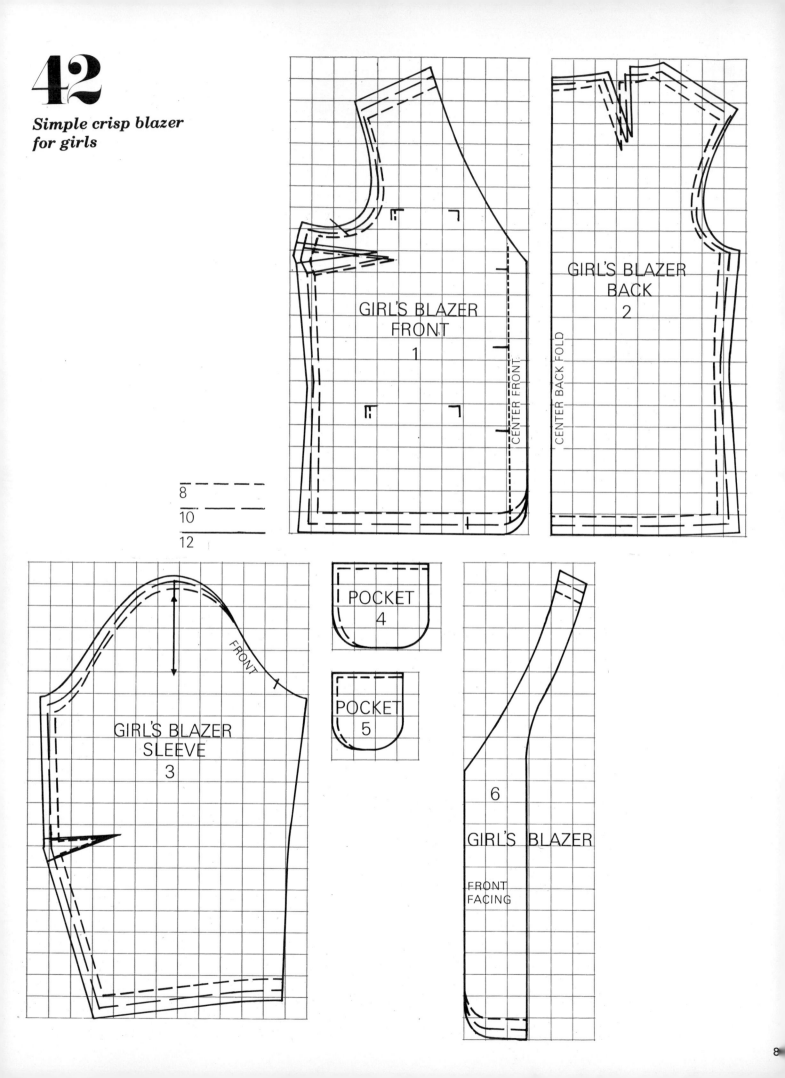

42

*Simple crisp blazer
for girls*

GIRL'S BLAZER
FRONT
1

CENTER FRONT

GIRL'S BLAZER
BACK
2

CENTER BACK FOLD

8
10
12

GIRL'S BLAZER
SLEEVE
3

FRONT

POCKET
4

POCKET
5

6

GIRL'S BLAZER

FRONT
FACING

43

Boy's blazer

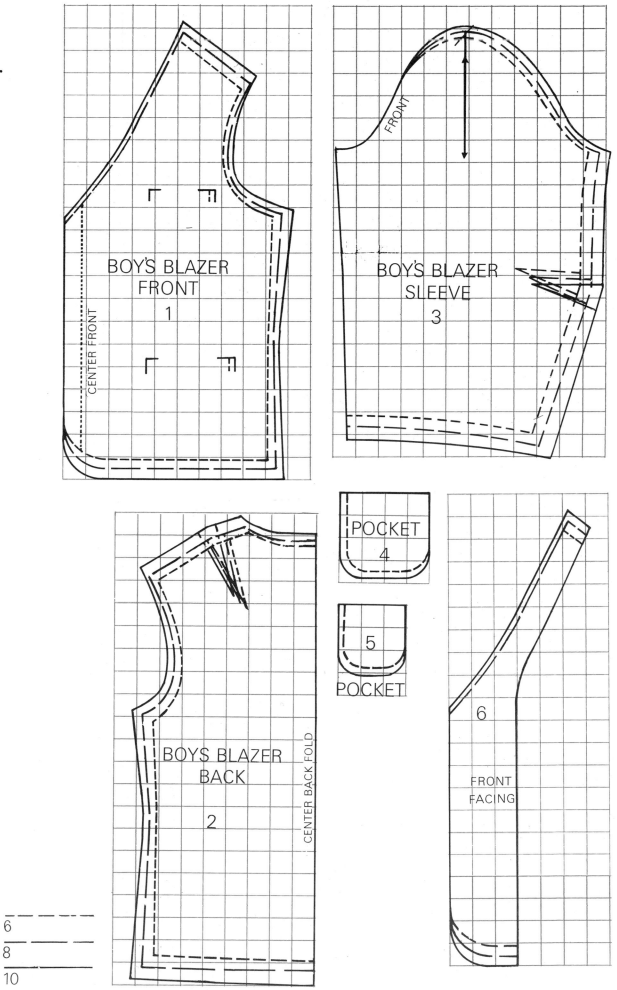

BOY'S BLAZER
FRONT

1

CENTER FRONT

BOY'S BLAZER
SLEEVE

3

FRONT

BOY'S BLAZER
BACK

2

CENTER BACK FOLD

POCKET
4

5
POCKET

6

FRONT
FACING

6
8
10

44

Party dress with frilly skirt and lace trimming

Fabric required

Sizes	3	5	yrs
45 inch fabric	$1\frac{1}{4}$	$1\frac{3}{8}$	yds
$1\frac{1}{4}$ inch wide eyelet lace	3	$3\frac{1}{4}$	yds
$\frac{3}{8}$ inch wide velvet ribbon	$1\frac{1}{2}$	$1\frac{1}{2}$	yds
Zipper	12	12	ins

To make pattern

See Know-how.

To cut out

See Know-how and follow the cutting lay-out. Place skirt 3 twice to fold. Remember the pattern has no hem or seam allowances so add these when cutting out. Allow $\frac{1}{2}$ inch turning only for skirt hem. No turnings are necessary at neck edge of dress. Allow $\frac{1}{2}$ inch turnings on bias strip for neck band.

Making up

Stitch darts, shoulder and side seams of bodice, side seams of skirt. Stitch center back seam of bodice from lower edge to within $12\frac{1}{2}$ inches of neck edge for both sizes. Press. Gather top edge of skirt to fit lower edge of bodice. With right sides together baste skirt to bodice, adjusting gathers evenly. Stitch. Press turnings towards bodice. Insert zipper into center back opening (see Working Details). Bind neck edge with self bias binding taking $\frac{1}{2}$ inch turnings (see Working Details, second method). Stitch sleeve seams. Press. Stitch sleeves into armholes (see Working Details). Turn up sleeve and skirt hems and sew in place. Attach lace at hem line and just above waist seam line using a fine needle and thread and small prick stitches. Thread velvet ribbon through lace at waist line and fasten in bow at center front.

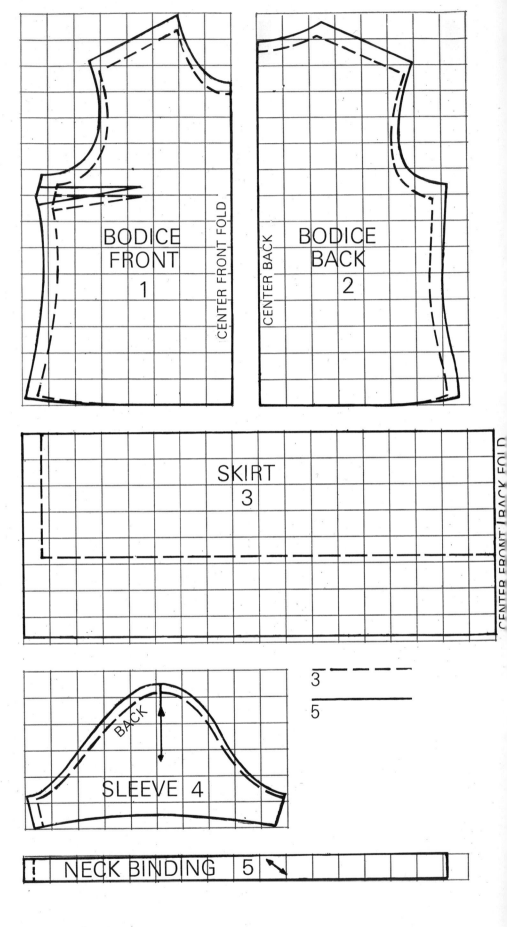

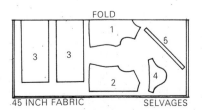

45

Short shirred dress with frilled collar

Fabric required

Sizes	4	6	8	yrs
36 inch fabric	$1\frac{7}{8}$	2	$2\frac{1}{8}$	yds
or				
45 inch fabric	$1\frac{3}{4}$	$1\frac{7}{8}$	$1\frac{7}{8}$	yds
Bias binding		$\frac{1}{2}$	$\frac{1}{2}$	$\frac{1}{2}$ yd
Zipper	14	14	16	ins
1 spool shirring elastic				

To make pattern
See Know-how.

To cut out
See Know-how and follow the cutting layout. Cut neck ruffle 4 in single fabric. Remember the pattern has no seam allowances so add these when cutting out. Allow $\frac{1}{2}$ inch hem only on sleeves and on one long and two short edges of neck ruffle.

Making up
Stitch darts. Press. Stitch side seams. Press. Shirr two rows of elastic $\frac{3}{8}$ inch apart along the three marked lines on dress backs and front (see Working Details). Stitch shoulder seams. Stitch center back seam from lower edge to within $14\frac{1}{2}$ inches of neck edge for sizes 4 and 6 and $16\frac{1}{2}$ inches for size 8 years. Press. Insert zipper in back opening (see Working Details). Turn in narrow hem on one long and two short edges of neck ruffle and slip stitch or machine zigzag in place. Gather ruffle to fit neck edge. Place to neck edge, right sides together, neatened ends to back opening of dress. Baste and stitch. Trim seam. Press turnings towards dress. Bind neck seam allowance with bias binding (see Working Details). Stitch sleeve seam. Press. Turn up sleeve hem and slip stitch or machine zigzag in place. Shirr two rows of elastic $\frac{3}{8}$ inch apart, the lower row $1\frac{3}{8}$ inches from hem line of sleeve. Stitch sleeve into armhole (see Working Details). Turn up hem of dress and slip stitch in place.

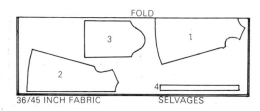

36/45 INCH FABRIC   SELVAGES

46

Boy's vest and pants

Fabric required

Sizes	6	8	10	yrs
60 inch fabric (pants)	1	$1\frac{1}{8}$	$1\frac{1}{8}$	yds
60 inch fabric (vest)	1	$1\frac{1}{8}$	$1\frac{1}{8}$	yds
36 inch lining	$1\frac{1}{4}$	$1\frac{1}{4}$	$1\frac{1}{4}$	yds
Interfacing	$\frac{1}{2}$	$\frac{1}{2}$	$\frac{1}{2}$	yd
Zipper	6	6	6	ins
Buttons	6	6	6	
Hooks and eyes				

To make pattern
See Know-how, also for patterns for back, neck and armhole facings (taper facings to 1 inch wide at shoulders).

To cut out
See Know-how and follow cutting layouts. Remember the pattern has no hem or seam allowances so add these when cutting out. Note the following. Vest: open out fabric to cut belt in single fabric. Pants: hem allowance already included on pattern and finished pants will be $4\frac{3}{8}$ inches shorter than pattern. Measure child carefully before cutting out and alter pattern if necessary. Cut lining as vest, omitting facings and pockets. Cut pants pockets four times in lining. Cut interfacing to shape of front facing.

Making up
Vest: Baste interfacing to front (see Working Details). Stitch darts, side and shoulder seams. Press. Stitch neck, front and armhole facings to vest (see Working Details). Turn up hem. Slip stitch lower edge of facing over hem turning. Topstitch $\frac{1}{2}$ inch from neck, front and lower edges. Turn in seam allowances of belt all round and baste. Position belt on garment and topstitch in place $\frac{1}{2}$ inch from edges. Fold each pocket piece in half along fold line, right sides together, and stitch round curved edges, leaving small opening to turn through. Turn right side out, slip stitch opening to close and press. Position on fronts and topstitch in position $\frac{1}{2}$ inch round sides and lower edge. Work machine or hand buttonholes in left front $\frac{7}{8}$ inch in from front edge, 2 inches apart, the bottom buttonhole in the center of the belt. Sew on buttons to correspond on both left and right fronts. Stitch lining and insert (see Working Details).

Pants: To make up pants and also to insert zipper with zipper guard and pockets see Working Details. Leave $6\frac{1}{2}$ inch opening for zipper at center front. Fold waist band lengthways, right sides together, and stitch across ends. Trim seam, turn right side out and press. Place one end to opening at left side and stitch one layer to waist with the right end extending $1\frac{1}{8}$ inch to form wrap. Slip stitch other long edge of waist band to inside over seam line turning in edges at wrap also. Fasten with hooks and eyes. Turn under pants ends along fold line ($2\frac{3}{4}$ inches from lower edge of pants) and slip stitch in place. Fold turn-up $1\frac{5}{8}$ inch to outside and press in place.

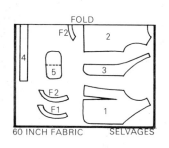

60 INCH FABRIC   SELVAGES

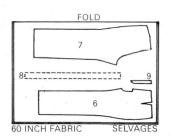

60 INCH FABRIC   SELVAGES

45

*Short shirred dress
with frilled collar*

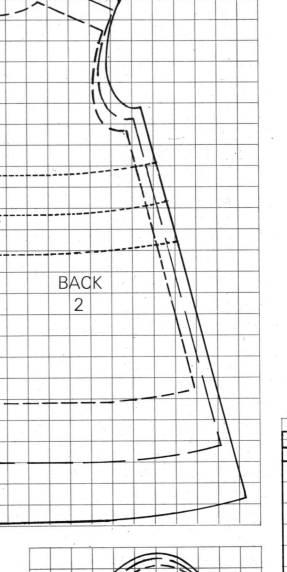

BACK
2

CENTER BACK

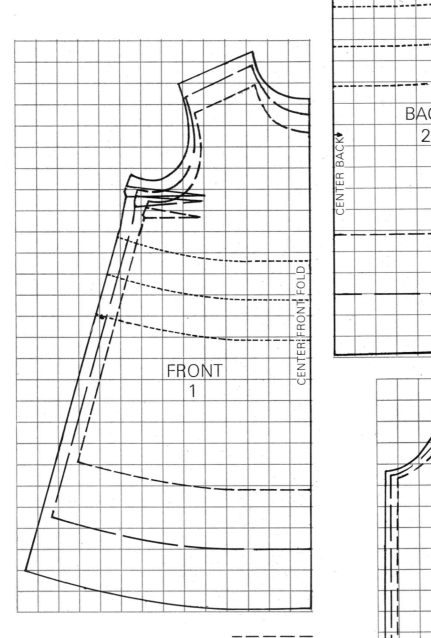

FRONT
1

CENTER FRONT FOLD

4

6

8

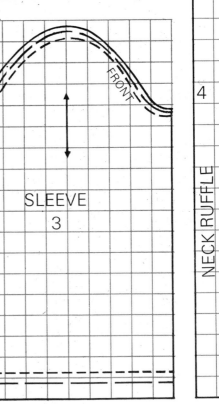

SLEEVE
3

FRONT

NECK RUFFLE

4

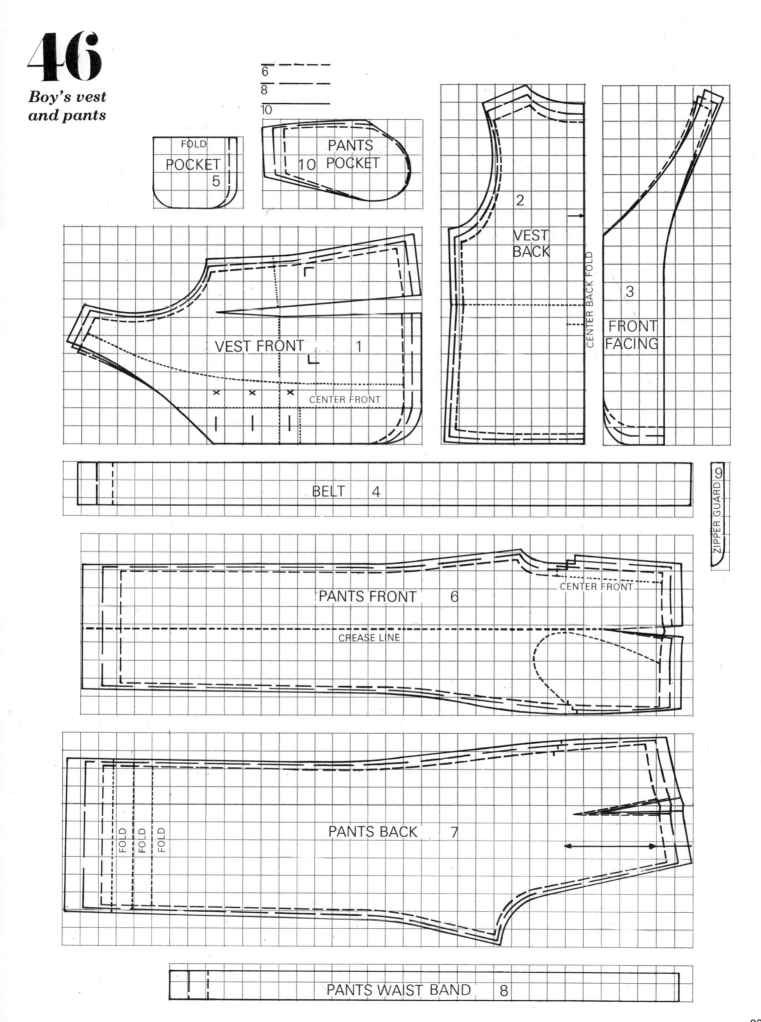

46

Boy's vest and pants

FOLD
POCKET
5

PANTS
POCKET
10

2
VEST
BACK

CENTER BACK FOLD

3
FRONT
FACING

VEST FRONT   1

CENTER FRONT

BELT   4

ZIPPER GUARD 9

PANTS FRONT   6

CENTER FRONT

CREASE LINE

PANTS BACK   7

FOLD FOLD FOLD

PANTS WAIST BAND   8

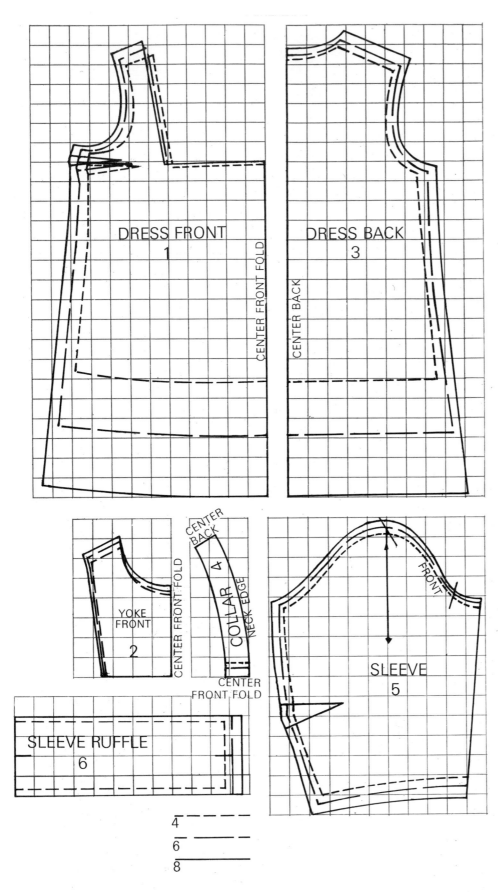

47

Gaily trimmed dress for a little girl

Fabric required

Sizes	4	6	8	yrs
36 inch fabric	$1\frac{3}{4}$	$1\frac{7}{8}$	2	yds
Narrow rick-rack braid	$4\frac{1}{2}$	$4\frac{3}{4}$	5	yds
Zipper	9	9	10	ins
Hooks and eyes	2	2	2	

To make pattern

See Know-how.

To cut out

See Know-how and follow the cutting layout. Place collar 4 twice to fold of fabric. Remember the pattern has no hem or seam allowances so add these when cutting out.

Making up

Gather top edge of dress front and draw up to fit lower edge of yoke insert. Adjust gathers evenly. With right sides together stitch insert to front. Snip into corners and press towards yoke. Stitch front darts and sleeve darts. Press. Stitch side, shoulder and sleeve seams. Press. Stitch center back seam from lower edge to within $9\frac{1}{2}$ inches of neck edge for sizes 4 and 6 and $10\frac{1}{2}$ inches for size 8 years. Press. Insert zipper into back opening (see Working Details). Make up and attach collar (see Working Details). Stitch short seam on each sleeve ruffle, right sides together, to make circles. Fold lengthways, wrong sides facing, gather long edges together and stitch to lower edge of sleeves. Press turnings towards sleeves. Stitch two rows of rick-rack to sleeves just above ruffles. Use small machine stitch or neat prick stitches. Stitch sleeves into armholes (see Working Details). Turn up hem and slip stitch in place. Stitch two rows of rick-rack above hem line. Trim the insert and collar with rick-rack as shown. Fasten collar with hooks and eyes.

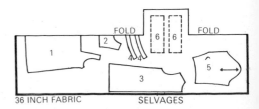

48

Little girl's smock dress

Fabric required

Sizes	4	6	yrs
36 inch fabric	$1\frac{3}{4}$	2	yds
or			
54 inch fabric	$1\frac{1}{4}$	$1\frac{3}{8}$	yds
Interfacing	$\frac{1}{2}$	$\frac{1}{2}$	yd
Small buttons	6	6	

To make pattern

See Know-how.

To cut out

See Know-how and follow the cutting layout. Cut pieces 5, 6 and 8 twice on double fabric. Cut interfacing for collar, neck band, fronts and cuffs. Remember the pattern has no hem or seam allowances so add these when cutting out.

Making up

Gather top edge of dress back to fit back yoke and stitch. Similarly gather top edge of dress front between markings and stitch to yoke front. Press turnings towards yokes. Stitch side and shoulder seams. Press. Baste interfacing to wrong side of one collar piece, one neck band and to fold line of each front. Catch stitch to front fold (see Working Details). Turn front facing to inside and tack. Starting from the neck edge topstitch $\frac{1}{4}$ inch from fold line for $8\frac{1}{2}$ inches for size 4 and $9\frac{1}{4}$ inches for size 6 years. Similarly work another row of topstitching $1\frac{1}{4}$ inches from fold line. Then place right front over left front, center fronts coinciding, and continue topstitching to lower edge through all thicknesses. Stitch a collar piece to each neck band piece, matching center backs, curved end of bands extending at front. Press seam allowance down towards neck band. Treat collar and neck band together as one piece and make up and attach to neck edge (see Working Details). Topstitch $\frac{1}{4}$ inch from outer edge of collar. Make lapped opening at lower edge of sleeve $1\frac{1}{4}$ inches wide, 6 inches from front edge of sleeve (see Working Details). Stitch sleeve seams. Press. Baste interfacing to two cuff pieces. Stitch each interfaced cuff to plain cuff piece at one long edge. Attach cuffs to lower edges of sleeves (see Working Details). Topstitch $\frac{1}{4}$ inch from all edges of cuff. Stitch sleeves into armholes (see Working Details). Topstitch $\frac{1}{4}$ inch inside all yoke seam lines. Work one machine or hand buttonhole in right front on neck band, one on yoke $1\frac{3}{8}$ inch from neck line, and two on each cuff, on the ends furthest from sleeve seams. Sew on corresponding buttons. Turn up hem and sew in place.

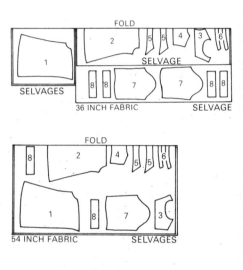

49

Boy's tucked shirt with stand-up collar

Fabric required

Sizes	6	8	yrs
36 inch fabric			
or			
45 inch fabric	$1\frac{3}{8}$	$1\frac{3}{8}$	yds
Small shirt buttons	9	9	

To make pattern

See Know-how.

To cut out

See Know-how and follow the cutting layout. Cut collar 5 twice on double fabric. Remember the pattern has no hem or seam allowances so add these when cutting out.

Making up

Fold fronts along tuck lines and stitch $\frac{1}{4}$ inch from folds. Press tucks towards sleeves. To make front bands stitch a front facing to each front. Press turnings towards facing. Fold facing to inside $1\frac{1}{8}$ inch from seam line. Topstitch $\frac{1}{4}$ inch from fold. Turn in seam allowance on inner edge and slip stitch to seam line. Work another row of topstitching $\frac{1}{4}$ inch from seam line. Stitch side and shoulder seams. Press. Stitch center back seam of both collar pieces, make up collar and attach to neck edge (see Working Details). Topstitch $\frac{1}{4}$ inch from all edges of collar. Make a lapped opening at lower edge of sleeve, $1\frac{1}{2}$ inches wide, 6 inches from front edge of sleeve (see Working Details). Stitch sleeve seam. Press. Attach cuff to sleeve (see Working Details). Stitch sleeve into armhole (see Working Details). Turn up hem and slip stitch in place. Make 6 vertical buttonholes on left front, 2 inches apart and $\frac{1}{2}$ inch in from fold. Make one horizontal buttonhole centrally on left side of collar, $\frac{1}{2}$ inch from front edge and one buttonhole on each cuff, on the ends furthest from sleeve seams. Attach corresponding buttons.

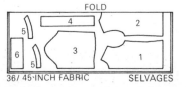

48

*Little girl's
smock dress*

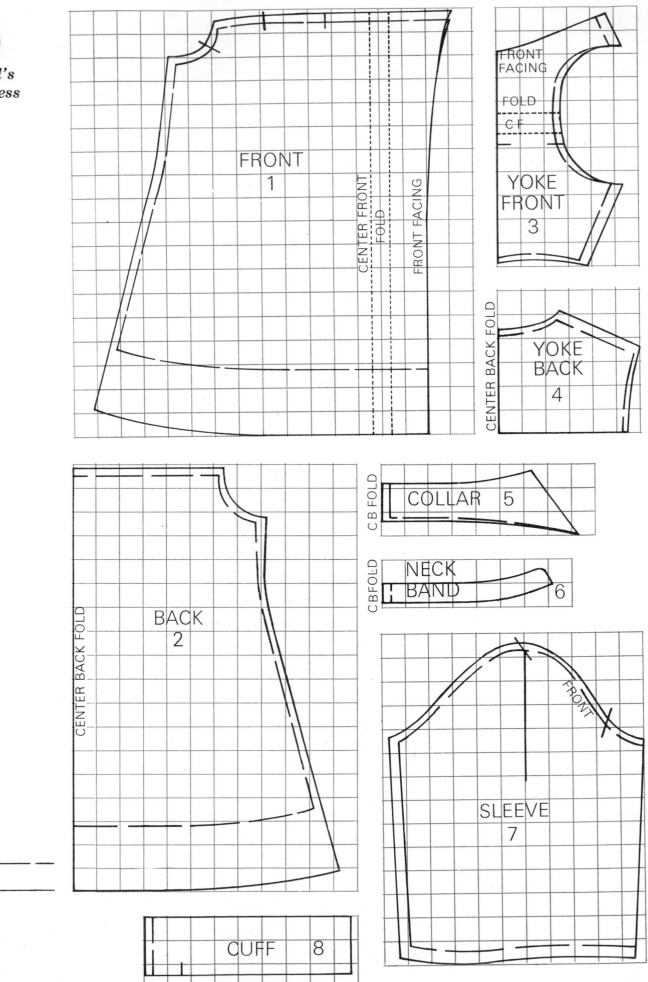

FRONT
1

CENTER FRONT FOLD

FRONT FACING

FRONT
FACING

FOLD

C F

YOKE
FRONT
3

CENTER BACK FOLD

YOKE
BACK
4

CB FOLD

COLLAR 5

CBFOLD

NECK
BAND 6

CENTER BACK FOLD

BACK
2

4
6

FRONT

SLEEVE
7

CUFF 8

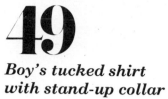

49

**Boy's tucked shirt
with stand-up collar**

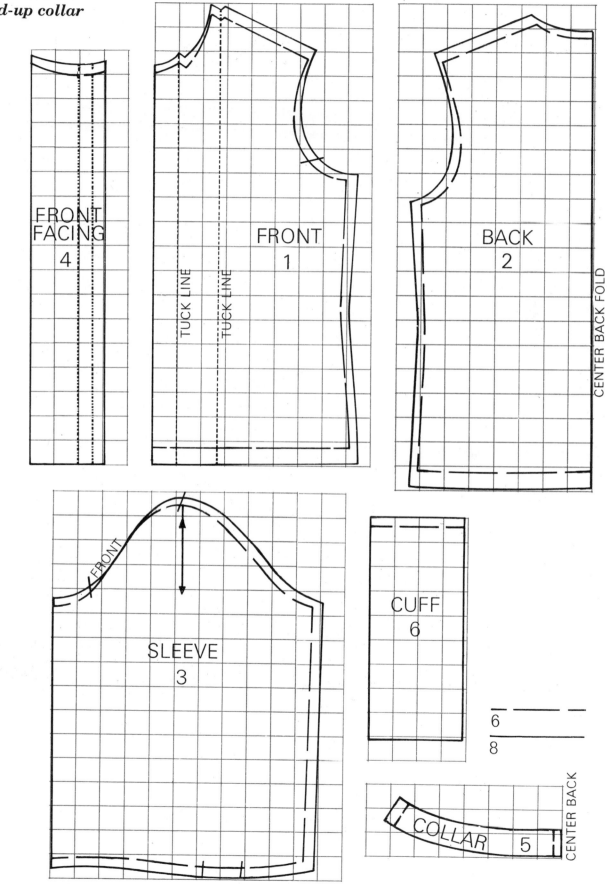

FRONT
FACING
4

FRONT
1

TUCK LINE

TUCK LINE

BACK
2

CENTER BACK FOLD

FRONT

SLEEVE
3

CUFF
6

6
8

COLLAR 5

CENTER BACK

50

*Girl's dress
with full flared skirt
and braid trimming*

Fabric required

Sizes	9	11	13	yrs
54 inch fabric	$1\frac{7}{8}$	2	$2\frac{1}{8}$	yds
$\frac{1}{2}$ inch wide rick-rack braid	4	$4\frac{1}{8}$	$4\frac{1}{4}$	yds
$\frac{1}{8}$ inch wide soutache braid	$3\frac{3}{8}$	$3\frac{1}{2}$	$3\frac{5}{8}$	yds
Zipper	16	16	18	ins
1 spool shirring elastic				

To make pattern

See Know-how, also for patterns for neck facings.

To cut out

See Know-how and follow the cutting layout. Remember the pattern has no hem or seam allowances so add these when cutting out. Allow $\frac{3}{4}$ inch hem only on sleeves, and 2 inches on skirt.

Making up

Stitch darts, shoulder and side seams of bodice and side seams of skirt. Press. Stitch skirt to bodice, with right sides together, matching seams. Press. Stitch neck facings (see Working Details). Stitch center back seam from lower edge to within $16\frac{1}{2}$ inches of neck seam edge for sizes 9 and 11 and $18\frac{1}{2}$ inches for size 13 years. Press. Insert zipper (see Working Details). Stitch sleeve seam. Press. Turn up sleeve hem. Shirr two rows of elastic $\frac{3}{8}$ inch apart at wrist, the first row 2 inches from hem. Stitch sleeve into armhole (see Working Details). Turn up skirt hem and sew in place (see Working Details). Sew on soutache braid and rick-rack with small prick stitches to dress neck, sleeves and hem as illustrated.

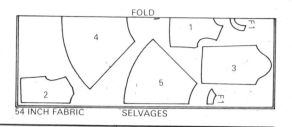

51

A bold tunic, gaily trimmed with rick-rack and cord

Fabric required

Sizes	8	10	12	yrs
45 inch fabric or				
54 inch fabric	$1\frac{3}{8}$	$1\frac{1}{2}$	$1\frac{1}{2}$	yds
$\frac{3}{8}$ inch wide rick-rack braid	$2\frac{1}{4}$	$2\frac{3}{8}$	$2\frac{1}{2}$	yds
$\frac{1}{4}$ inch wide cord	$2\frac{1}{2}$	$2\frac{5}{8}$	$2\frac{3}{4}$	yds
Zipper	14	16	16	ins
Hooks and eyes				

To make pattern
See Know-how.

To cut out
See Know-how and follow the cutting layout, cutting collar twice in double fabric. Remember the pattern has no hem or seam allowances so add these when cutting out.

Making up
Stitch darts. Press. Stitch side seams from armhole edge for $9\frac{5}{8}$ inches for size 8, $10\frac{3}{8}$ inches for size 10 and $11\frac{1}{8}$ inches for size 12 years. Press. Turn seam allowances of side slit openings to inside and press along fold. Slip stitch in place. Stitch shoulder seams. Stitch center back seam from lower edge to within $14\frac{1}{2}$ inches of neck edge for size 8 and $16\frac{1}{2}$ inches for other sizes. Press. Insert zipper in center back seam (see Working Details). Make up the two collar halves and attach to neck edge with rounded ends to center front (see Working Details). Stitch sleeve darts. Press down. Stitch sleeve seams. Press. Stitch sleeves into armholes (see Working Details). Turn up hem of sleeves

and tunic. Sew on rick-rack braid with small prick stitches and slip stitch cord in place as illustrated (see back view). Fasten back of collar with two hooks and eyes.

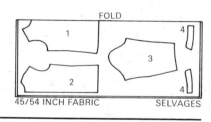

52

Boy's cossack tunic, belted and trimmed with fancy ribbon

Fabric required

Sizes	4	6	8	yrs
45 inch fabric or	$1\frac{1}{2}$	$1\frac{1}{2}$	$1\frac{5}{8}$	yds
54 inch fabric	$1\frac{3}{8}$	$1\frac{3}{8}$	$1\frac{1}{2}$	yds
$\frac{5}{8}$ inch wide fancy ribbon or braid	3	$3\frac{1}{8}$	$3\frac{1}{4}$	yds
36 inch interfacing	$\frac{1}{2}$	$\frac{1}{2}$	$\frac{3}{4}$	yd
Snap fasteners	10	10	10	
1 buckle				

To make pattern
See Know-how.

To cut out
See Know-how and follow the cutting layouts, placing collar 5 twice to fold. Open out fabric to cut belt in single fabric. Cut interfacing for collar, front bands and cuffs. Remember the pattern has no hem or seam allowances so add these when cutting out.

Making up
Baste interfacing to wrong side of one half of each front band and each cuff, and to one collar piece (see Working Details). Catch stitch to fold where applicable. Stitch yoke to back. Stitch side and shoulder seams. Press. Make up collar, leaving front edges open and attach to neck edge (see Working Details). Fold front bands in half lengthways, right sides together, and stitch across top ends. Turn right side out and press. With right sides together place interfaced edge of front bands to each front, top edge of band level with top edge of collar. Stitch in place to collar and fronts, stitching interfaced half of band only. Press turnings towards bands. Fold in seam allowance on inside and slip stitch in place over seam line. Topstitch $\frac{1}{4}$ inch from all edges of collar and front bands. Make three pleats at lower edge of sleeves, placing line onto adjacent arrow. Baste in place. Stitch sleeve seam. Press. Working on each cuff stitch short edges of cuff together to form circle, right sides together. Stitch interfaced half to lower edge of sleeve. Press turnings towards cuff. Turn non-interfaced half to inside, turn in seam allowance and slip stitch in place over seam line. Press. Stitch sleeve into armhole (see Working Details). Turn up

hem of tunic and slip stitch in place. Sew two rows of braid onto tunic $\frac{1}{8}$ inch apart, from shoulder to hem, the first row starting where neck line meets shoulder. Trim both edges of cuff with braid. Fasten the front with snap fasteners. Make the belt (see Working Details).

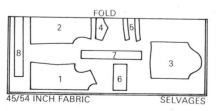

50

Girl's dress
with full flared skirt
and braid trimming

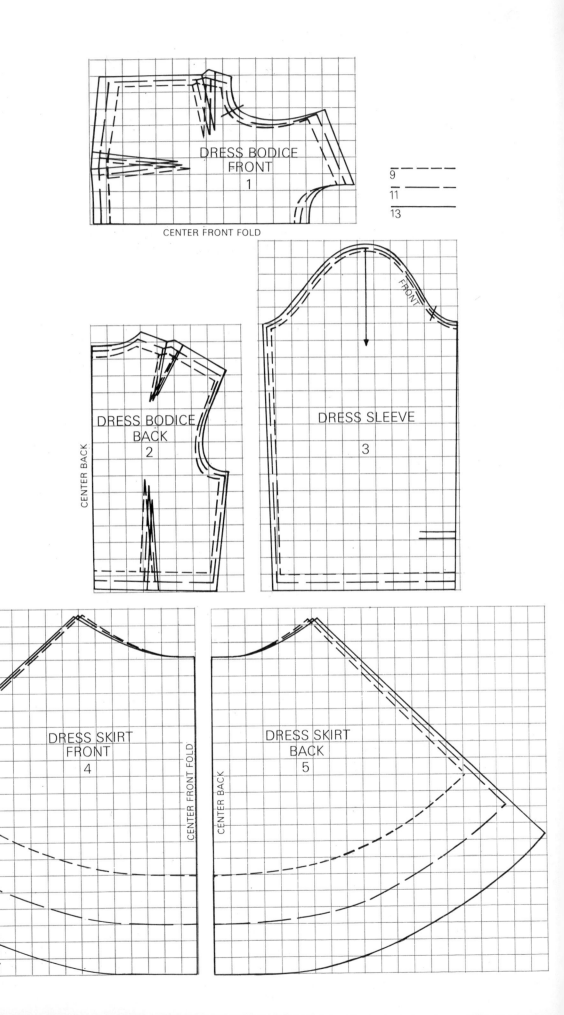

DRESS BODICE
FRONT
1

CENTER FRONT FOLD

9
11
13

DRESS BODICE
BACK
2

CENTER BACK

DRESS SLEEVE
3

FRONT

DRESS SKIRT
FRONT
4

CENTER FRONT FOLD

DRESS SKIRT
BACK
5

CENTER BACK

*A bold tunic,
gaily trimmed with
rick-rack and cord*

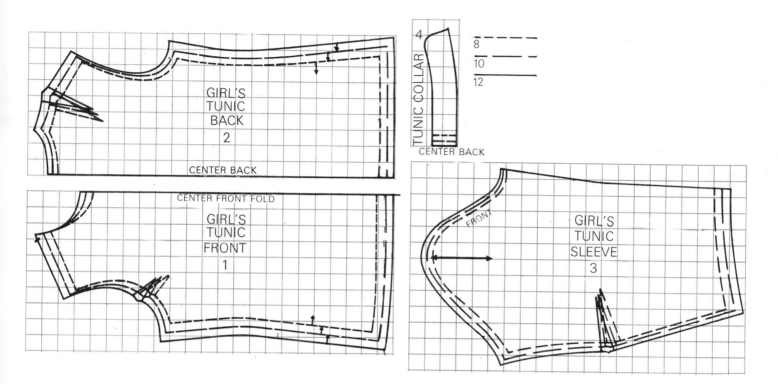

GIRL'S
TUNIC
BACK
2

CENTER BACK

TUNIC COLLAR

4

8
10
12

CENTER BACK

CENTER FRONT FOLD

GIRL'S
TUNIC
FRONT
1

GIRL'S
TUNIC
SLEEVE
3

FRONT

52

*Boy's cossack tunic,
belted and trimmed
with fancy ribbon*

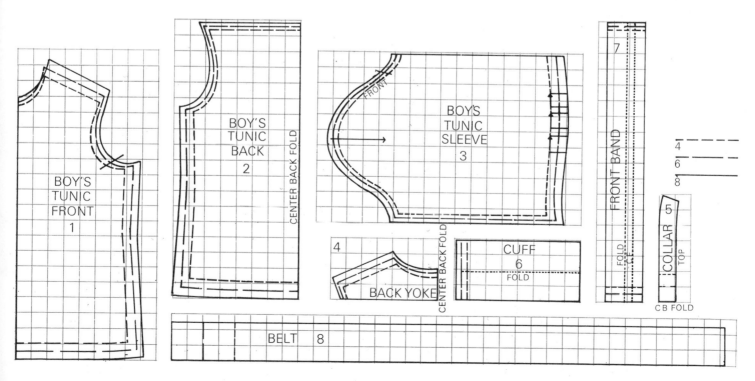

BOY'S
TUNIC
FRONT
1

BOY'S
TUNIC
BACK
2

CENTER BACK FOLD

BOY'S
TUNIC
SLEEVE
3

FRONT

7

FRONT BAND

FOLD

4
6
8

COLLAR
5

TOP

4

BACK YOKE

CENTER BACK FOLD

CUFF
6
FOLD

CB FOLD

BELT   8

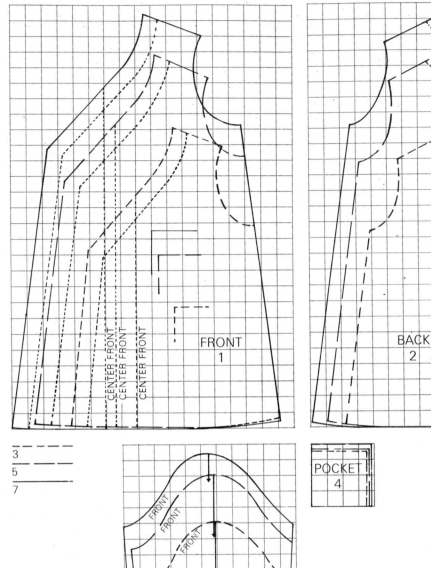

FRONT
1

CENTER FRONT
CENTER FRONT
CENTER FRONT

BACK
2

CENTER BACK FOLD

3
5
7

SLEEVE
3

FRONT
FRONT
FRONT

POCKET
4

53

*Judo-style
dressing gown
for boy or girl*

Fabric required

Sizes	3	5	7	yrs
45 inch fabric or				
54 inch fabric	$1\frac{1}{2}$	$1\frac{5}{8}$	$1\frac{3}{4}$	yds
36 or 45 inch				
contrast fabric	$\frac{3}{4}$	$\frac{7}{8}$	1	yd

To make pattern

See Know-how, also for patterns for 1 inch wide neck and front facings.

To cut out

See Know-how and follow cutting layouts. Remember the pattern has no hem or seam allowances so add these when cutting out. Cut facings with seam allowances all round. No hem allowance is needed on sleeve so check length before cutting. Cut belt in double fabric $3\frac{1}{2}$ inches wide 24 inches long for size 3, 26 inches long for size 5 and 28 inches long for size 7 years (this includes turnings). Cut strips in double fabric 1 inch wide to width of pocket and lower edge of sleeve (add turnings).

Making up

Stitch side, shoulder and sleeve seams. Stitch back and front neck facings at shoulder seams. Press. Place neck and front facings to inside of neck line, matching shoulder seams, with right side of facing meeting wrong side of garment. Stitch. Press, layer and clip seam allowance. Turn facing to outside. Turn in outer edge of facing, clipping carefully at curves and corners, and slip stitch in place. Press. Stitch shorter edges of each sleeve band together to make circle. Press. Stitch to lower edge of sleeve as for neck facing. Stitch sleeve into armhole (see Working Details). Attach bands to upper edge of pockets as for neck facing, also stitch narrow ends of band as far as lower seam allowance before turning band to right side of pocket. Snip seam allowance at end of stitching. Trim and layer seam allowances then turn band to right side. Turn in seam allowance at sides and lower edge of pockets and slip stitch in place. Position and slip stitch or top-stitch in place $\frac{1}{8}$ inch from side and lower edges. Turn up hem and slip stitch in place. Make up tie belt (see Working Details) omitting buckle.

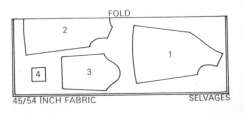

FOLD

2

4

3

1

45/54 INCH FABRIC   SELVAGES

54

Girl's doubled breasted vest and pants

Fabric required

Sizes	3	5	7	yrs
36 inch fabric	$2\frac{3}{4}$	$2\frac{7}{8}$	3	yds
or				
54 inch fabric	$1\frac{1}{2}$	$1\frac{5}{8}$	$1\frac{5}{8}$	yds
36 inch lining	$1\frac{3}{8}$	$1\frac{3}{8}$	$1\frac{1}{2}$	yds
or				
54 inch lining	$\frac{3}{4}$	$\frac{3}{4}$	$\frac{3}{4}$	yd
Zipper	6	6	6	ins
Buttons	6	6	6	
Interfacing	$\frac{1}{2}$	$\frac{1}{2}$	$\frac{1}{2}$	yd
Hooks and eyes				

To make pattern

See Know-how, also for making patterns for neck and armhole facings. Front neck facing to join the folded back front bodice facing.

To cut out

See Know-how and follow the cutting layouts. Cut waist band 5 in two pieces, placing twice to fold to make up full length. Cut lining as vest, omitting facings. Cut interfacing as facings. Remember the pattern has no hem or seam allowances so add these when cutting out.

Making up

Vest: Baste interfacing to inside of fronts and front and back neck edges (see Working Details). Stitch darts, side and shoulder seams. Press. Stitch neck and armhole facings (see Working Details). Make 3 buttonholes $2\frac{3}{4}$ inches apart in right front with outer edge of buttonholes $\frac{5}{8}$ inch from front fold line, top one $\frac{5}{8}$ inch from top edge. Sew on corresponding buttons on both left and right fronts. Turn up hem and sew in place. Make up lining and insert (see Working Details).

Pants: To make up and also to insert zipper see Working Details. Leave $6\frac{1}{2}$ inch opening for zipper at center front. Fold waist band in half and stitch across ends. Turn right side out and press. Place one end to center front opening at right side and stitch one layer to waist with the left end extending to form wrap. Slip stitch waist band to inside. Fasten with hooks and eyes. Sew pants hems.

55

Girl's frilled blouse

Fabric required

Sizes	3	5	7	yrs
36 inch fabric	$1\frac{1}{4}$	$1\frac{1}{4}$	$1\frac{3}{8}$	yds
Small shirt buttons	7	7	7	
$\frac{1}{2}$ inch wide lace	$4\frac{1}{2}$	$4\frac{1}{2}$	$4\frac{1}{2}$	yds

To make pattern

See Know-how.

To cut out

See Know-how and follow the cutting layout. Fold collar 3 over and mark out the full shape before cutting out. Remember the pattern has no hem or seam allowances so add these when cutting out.

Making up

Stitch darts in back shoulder. Make up as for boy's shirt (no 26), making 5 evenly spaced buttonholes in right band, the top one $\frac{1}{2}$ inch from top edge.

56

Boy's vest and pants

Fabric required

Sizes	3	5	7	yrs
54 inch fabric	$1\frac{1}{4}$	$1\frac{1}{2}$	$1\frac{3}{8}$	yds
36 inch lining	$\frac{1}{2}$	$\frac{1}{2}$	$\frac{1}{2}$	yd
Zipper	6	6	6	ins
Interfacing	$\frac{1}{2}$	$\frac{1}{2}$	$\frac{1}{2}$	yd
Buttons	6	6	6	
Hooks and eyes				

To make pattern

See Know-how, also for making patterns for neck and armhole facings. As shoulder is narrow make front neck and armhole facing in one, back neck and armhole facing in one. Front neck facing to join the folded back front bodice facing.

To cut out

See Know-how and follow the cutting layouts. Cut the zipper guard 6 once from fabric and once from lining. Cut waist band 5 from single fabric. Cut vest lining as vest omitting facings. Cut interfacing for front and neck facings. Remember the pattern has no hem or seam allowance so add these when cutting out.

Making up

Vest: Baste interfacing to inside of fronts and front and back neck edges. Stitch darts and side seams. Press. Stitch neck and armhole facings at side seams then stitch to garment (see Working Details) stopping the stitching $1\frac{1}{2}$ inches from shoulders. Clip seams and turn right side out. Press. Stitch shoulder seams of vest. Turn in shoulder seams of facings to meet and slip stitch remainder of neck and armhole edges. Turn up hem and sew in place. Make 3 evenly spaced buttonholes in left front with outer edge of buttonholes $\frac{5}{8}$ inch from front fold line, top one $\frac{5}{8}$ inch from top edge. Sew on corresponding buttons on both right and left fronts. Make up lining and insert (see Working Details).

Pants: To make and also to insert zipper with guard see Working Details, finishing front crotch seam at base of front extension. Fold waist band lengthways and stitch across ends. Turn right side out and press. Place one end to center front opening at left side and stitch one layer to waist, other end extending to form wrap. Slip stitch waist band to inside. Fasten with hooks and eyes. Stitch pants hems.

57

Boy's frilled shirt

Fabric required

Sizes	3	5	7	yrs
36 inch fabric	$1\frac{1}{4}$	$1\frac{1}{4}$	$1\frac{3}{8}$	yds
Buttons	6	6	6	
$\frac{1}{2}$ inch wide lace	$4\frac{1}{2}$	$4\frac{1}{2}$	$4\frac{1}{2}$	yds

To make pattern

See Know-how.

To cut out

See Know-how and follow the cutting layout. Fold collar 3 over and mark out the full shape before cutting out. Remember the pattern has no hem or seam allowances so add these when cutting out.

Making up

Gather and then stitch two rows of lace to each front, the first row $1\frac{1}{4}$ inches from front edge and the second row $1\frac{7}{8}$ inches from front edge. Working on each front, stitch right side of front band to wrong side of fronts down long edge. Also stitch at neck edge from seam to center front and snip into seam allowance at end of stitches. Turn band to right side and press seam allowance towards band. Turn in seam allowance along remaining long edge and slip stitch in place to first row of lace. Press. Stitch side and shoulder seams. Press. Stitch collar (see Working Details). The collar begins and ends at the center front of the band. Make 4 evenly spaced buttonholes in center of left front band, the top one $\frac{1}{2}$ inch from top edge. Make slashed openings at base of sleeves, $7\frac{3}{4}$ inches in from front edge (see Working Details). Stitch sleeve seam. Press. Gather lower edge of sleeve. Gather remaining lace and baste to sleeve along seam line $\frac{3}{4}$ inch from lower edge, to be included in seam with cuff. Stitch cuff (see Working Details). Stitch sleeve into armhole (see Working Details). Turn up the hem. Make buttonhole in each cuff. Sew on buttons to correspond.

54

*Girl's double breasted
vest and pants*

GIRL'S PANTS FRONT 3

CREASE LINE

GIRL'S VEST FRONT 1

CENTER FRONT

FOLD

GIRL'S VEST BACK 2

CENTER BACK FOLD

GIRL'S PANTS BACK 4

GIRL'S PANTS WAIST BAND 5

3
—
5
—
7

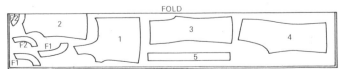

FOLD

F2 F1

F1

2

1

3

5

4

36 INCH FABRIC   SELVAGES

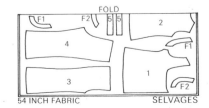

FOLD

F1 F2 5 5 2

4

F1

3

1

F2

54 INCH FABRIC   SELVAGES

55

Girl's frilled blouse

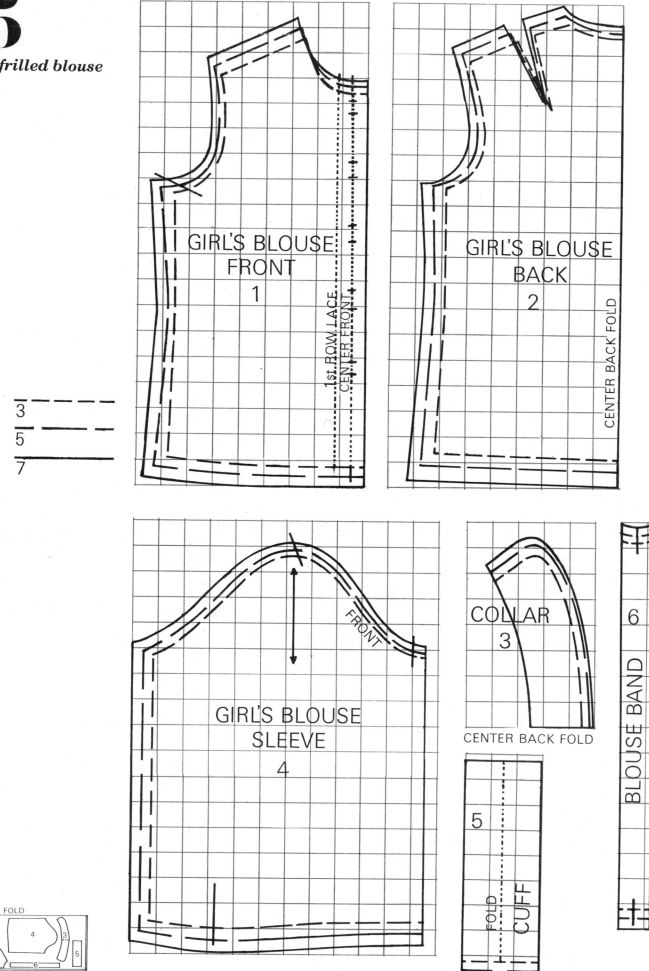

GIRL'S BLOUSE FRONT 1

1st ROW LACE

CENTER FRONT

GIRL'S BLOUSE BACK 2

CENTER BACK FOLD

3
5
7

GIRL'S BLOUSE SLEEVE 4

FRONT

COLLAR 3

CENTER BACK FOLD

BLOUSE BAND 6

5

FOLD

CUFF

FOLD

2

4

3

1

6

5

36 INCH FABRIC

SELVAGES

56

*Boy's vest
and pants*

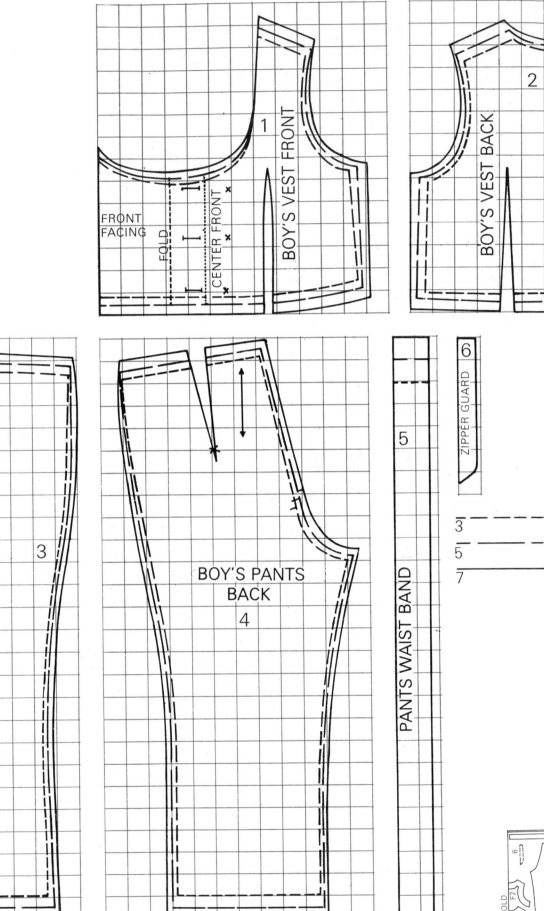

BOY'S VEST FRONT

1

FRONT
FACING

FOLD

CENTER FRONT

BOY'S VEST BACK

2

CENTER BACK FOLD

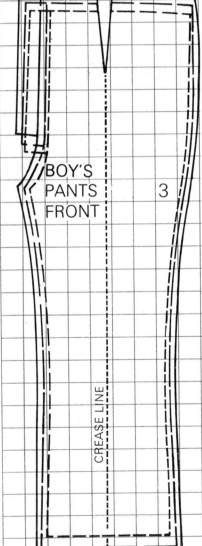

BOY'S
PANTS
FRONT

3

CREASE LINE

BOY'S PANTS
BACK

4

PANTS WAIST BAND

5

ZIPPER GUARD

6

3

5

7

54 INCH FABRIC

SELVAGES

FOLD

57

Boy's frilled shirt

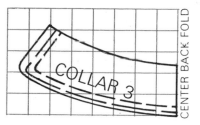

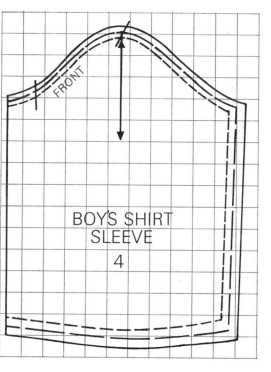

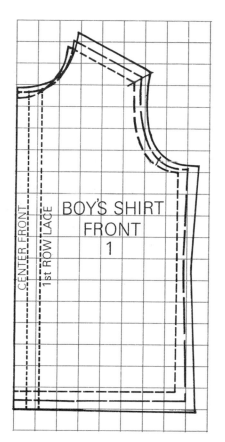

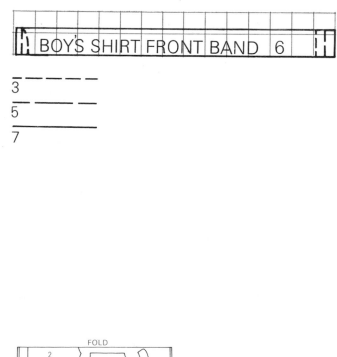

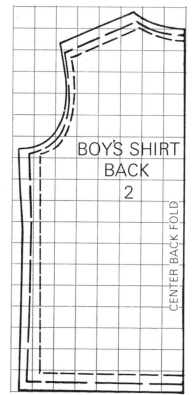

BOY'S SHIRT FRONT BAND   6

3
5
7

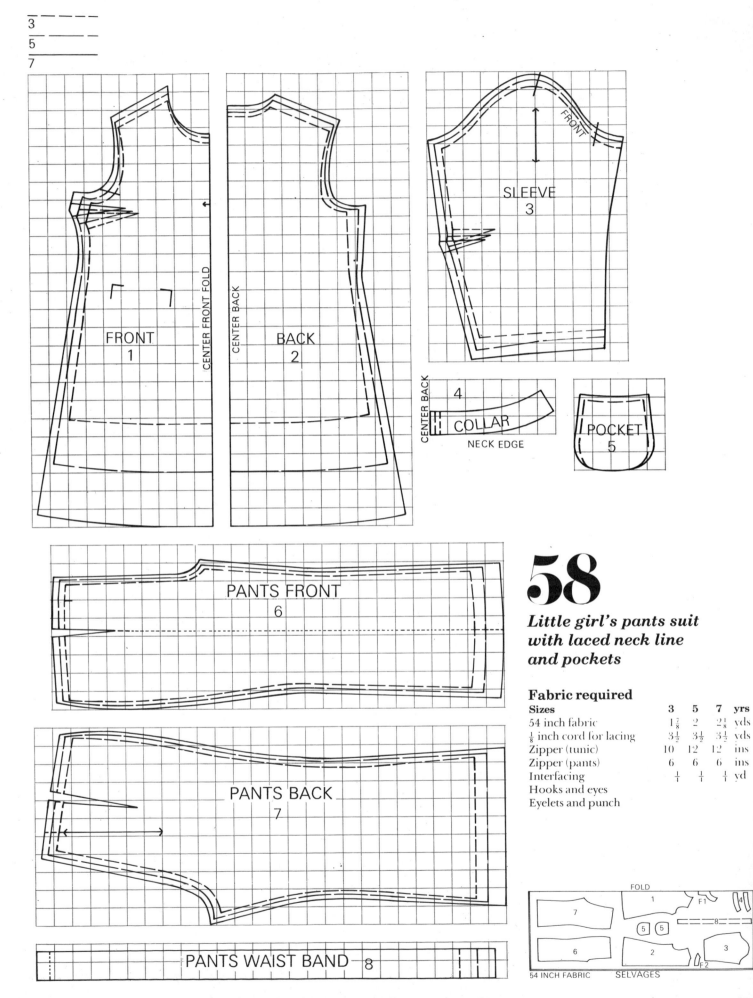

3
5
7

FRONT
1

CENTER FRONT FOLD

CENTER BACK

BACK
2

SLEEVE
3

FRONT

CENTER BACK

4 COLLAR

NECK EDGE

POCKET
5

PANTS FRONT
6

PANTS BACK
7

PANTS WAIST BAND 8

58

*Little girl's pants suit
with laced neck line
and pockets*

Fabric required

Sizes	3	5	7	yrs
54 inch fabric	$1\frac{7}{8}$	2	$2\frac{1}{8}$	yds
$\frac{1}{8}$ inch cord for lacing	$3\frac{1}{2}$	$3\frac{1}{2}$	$3\frac{1}{2}$	yds
Zipper (tunic)	10	12	12	ins
Zipper (pants)	6	6	6	ins
Interfacing	$\frac{1}{4}$	$\frac{1}{4}$	$\frac{1}{4}$	yd
Hooks and eyes				
Eyelets and punch				

FOLD

7

1

F1

4

5 5

8

6

2

3

F2

54 INCH FABRIC   SELVAGES

112

To make pattern

See Know-how, also for pattern for neck facings. Extend front neck facing down center front to $4\frac{1}{2}$ inches from neck line for size 3, $4\frac{3}{4}$ inches for size 5 and 5 inches for size 7 years.

To cut out

See Know-how and follow the cutting layouts. Cut out pocket 5 and collar 4 twice on double fabric. Cut out interfacing for collar and pockets. Remember the pattern has no hem or seam allowances so add these when cutting out.

Making up

Tunic: Baste interfacing to wrong side of one left and one right collar piece and use as top collars. Cut out a 2 inch wide strip of interfacing to length of front facing extension. Baste down center front. Baste front neck facing to front with right sides together. Starting at neck edge stitch $\frac{1}{4}$ inch from center front to slash mark, across base at right angles and back up other side $\frac{1}{4}$ inch from center front of neck line. Cut between stitching, clip into corners. Stitch darts in tunic and sleeves. Press. Stitch shoulder, side and sleeve seams. Press. Make up collars (see Working Details). Baste all thicknesses of collars to neck edge, front edges of collars to front opening, avoiding front facing. Join neck facings and stitch in place (see Working Details) over collars. Clip seam. Turn facing to inside and slip stitch to seam allowances. Stitch center back seam from lower edge to within $10\frac{1}{2}$ inches of neck edge for size 3, and $12\frac{1}{2}$ inches for sizes 5 and 7 years. Insert zipper into back opening (see Working Details). Baste interfacing to wrong side of two pocket pieces. The interfaced pieces will go to top of pockets. With right sides together stitch interfaced and plain pocket pieces in pairs, leaving small opening to turn through. Turn right side out, close openings and press. Punch 2 eyelets in pockets $1\frac{1}{2}$ inches from each side, $\frac{3}{4}$ inch from top. Topstitch pockets in position on front $\frac{1}{4}$ inch from edges. Punch 2 eyelets either side of front slash, $\frac{1}{2}$ inch from edge, top ones 1 inch from neck line, second ones $2\frac{1}{2}$ inches from neck line. Punch eyelets in center of collar fronts $\frac{1}{2}$ inch from edges. Stitch sleeves into armholes (see Working Details). Turn up hem of tunic and sleeves and sew in place. Thread cord through eyelet holes. Fasten back of collar with hook and eye.

Pants: To make up and insert zipper see Working Details. Leave $6\frac{1}{2}$ inch opening for zipper at center front. Fold waist band in half right sides together. Stitch across ends. Turn right side out and press. Place one end to center front opening at right side and stitch one layer to waist, the other end extending $\frac{3}{4}$ inch to form wrap. Slip stitch waist band to inside. Fasten with hooks and eyes. Sew pants hems.

59

The ideal winter coat, with fur trimmed hood

Fabric required

Sizes	5	7	9	yrs
54 inch fabric	$1\frac{1}{2}$	$1\frac{5}{8}$	$1\frac{3}{4}$	yds
36 inch lining	2	$2\frac{1}{8}$	$2\frac{1}{4}$	yds
2 inch wide fur fabric trim	$1\frac{3}{4}$	2	$2\frac{1}{8}$	yds
Open ended zipper	18	20	22	ins
Interfacing		$\frac{5}{8}$	$\frac{3}{4}$	$\frac{3}{4}$ yd

To make pattern
See Know-how.

To cut out
See Know-how and follow the cutting layout. Cut lining pattern as coat omitting facings. Cut interfacing to shape of front facing and also 2 inch wide strip to length of front edge of hood pieces. Remember the pattern has no hem or seam allowances so add these when cutting out.

Making up
Baste interfacing to wrong side of coat and hood fronts and catch along inner fold edges (see Working Details). Stitch darts in fronts and sleeves. Stitch side, sleeve and shoulder seams, easing back shoulder to fit front. Press. With right sides together stitch pocket sections to lining sections leaving small opening at lower edge to turn through. Turn right side out, slip stitch opening to close and press. Place on coat fronts and topstitch in position $\frac{1}{2}$ inch from side and lower edges. Working on hood join center to side sections. Press. Fold hood front facing to inside (see balance marks) and slip stitch in place. Baste hood to neck edge of coat, right sides together. Stitch hood in place (see Working Details for collar with facings). Fold front facing to inside and slip stitch in place. Insert zipper in front opening (see Working Details). Stitch sleeve into armhole (see Working Details). Turn up sleeve and coat hems and slip stitch or invisibly herringbone in place. Topstitch $\frac{1}{2}$ inch from sleeve hems. Slip stitch fur trimming in place around hood and down fronts. Make up lining and insert (see Working Details).

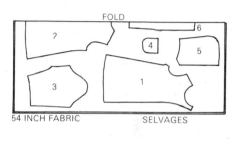

60

Boy's warm checked jacket and turn-up pants

Fabric required

Sizes	6	8	10	yrs
Jacket				
54 inch fabric	$1\frac{1}{8}$	$1\frac{1}{4}$	$1\frac{3}{8}$	yds
Fur fabric: 36 inch or				
45 inch or 54 inch	$\frac{1}{2}$	$\frac{1}{2}$	$\frac{1}{2}$	yd
36 inch lining	$1\frac{1}{8}$	$1\frac{3}{8}$	$1\frac{1}{2}$	yds
or 54 inch lining	1	$1\frac{1}{8}$	$1\frac{1}{8}$	yds
Open ended zipper	7	8	9	ins
Two sleeve zippers	4	4	4	ins
Interfacing	$\frac{1}{2}$	$\frac{1}{2}$	$\frac{1}{2}$	yd
Pants				
54 inch fabric	$1\frac{1}{4}$	$1\frac{3}{8}$	$1\frac{3}{8}$	yds
Zipper	6	6	6	ins
Hook and eye				

To make pattern
See Know-how, also for patterns for waist facings for pants. Close waist darts before tracing off facings.

To cut out
See Know-how and follow the cutting layouts. Cut zipper guard 11 once in fabric and once in lining. Cut pants pockets 10 four times in lining. Draw up the whole shape of collar 4 and cut on single fabric. Cut interfacing for front facing, lapel and collar. Remember the pattern has no hem or seam allowances so add these when cutting out. A 3 inch turn-up and 1 inch hem have already been allowed on pants. Check length carefully before cutting out.

Making up
Jacket: Stitch side and shoulder seams. Press. Baste interfacing to wrong side of front, lapel and collar. Join fur fabric lapel facings to front facings along straight edge, right sides together (when joined they make up shape of revers). Stitch front facing to front of jacket from upper end of crease line round collar flaps to lower edge of jacket. Make up collar and attach (see Working Details). Make slashed opening at base of sleeve 5 inches in from front edge of sleeve. Insert zippers into sleeve openings leaving teeth uncovered. Stitch sleeve darts and seams. Press. Stitch sleeves into armholes (see Working Details). Turn up sleeve and jacket hems. Insert open ended zipper in front (see Working Details) stitching right hand side of zipper 4 inches in from front edge of right jacket front and stitch left hand edge of zipper to left front edge of jacket.

Pants: To make pants and also to insert pockets and zipper with guard see Working Details. Leave $6\frac{1}{2}$ inch opening for zipper at center front. Stitch waist darts. Join side seams of waist facings. Place to waist edge, right sides together, matching seam lines, and stitch. Turn to inside and neaten front ends behind zipper. Fasten with hook and eye. Turn up pants along fold line (4 inches from lower edge) and slip stitch in place. Fold turn up 3 inches to outside and press in place. Then catch to seam lines.

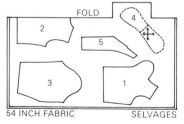

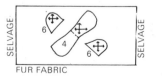

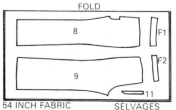

59

**The ideal winter coat,
with fur trimmed hood**

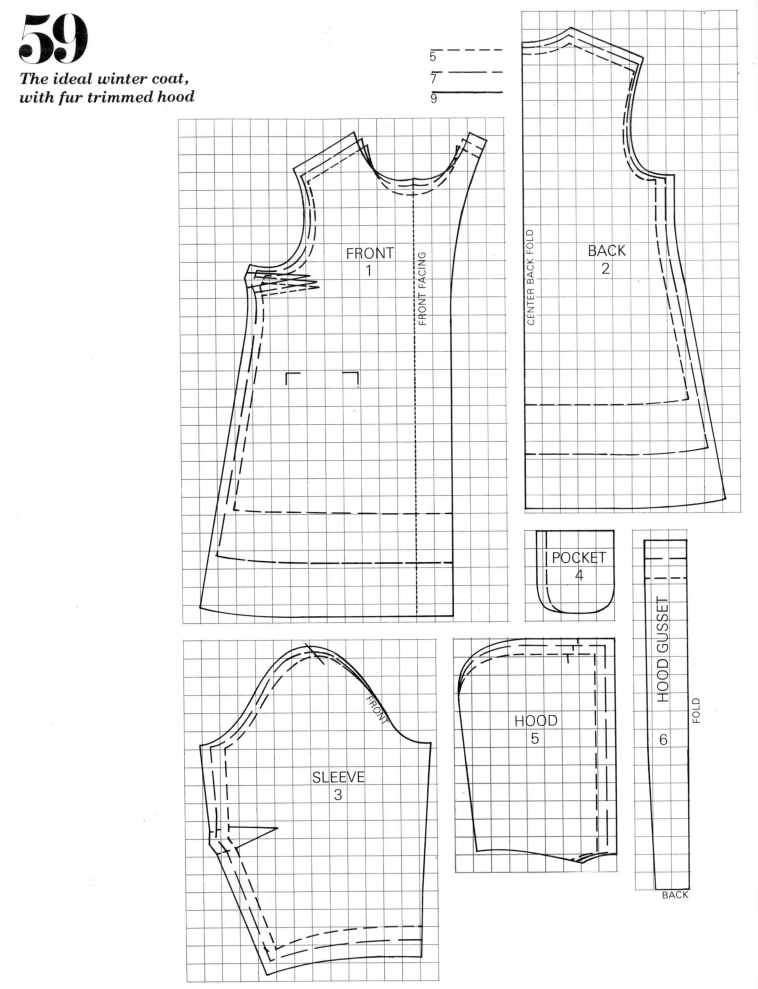

FRONT
1

FRONT FACING

CENTER BACK FOLD

BACK
2

POCKET
4

HOOD GUSSET

FOLD

6

SLEEVE
3

FRONT

HOOD
5

BACK

60

*Boy's warm checked jacket
and turn-up pants*

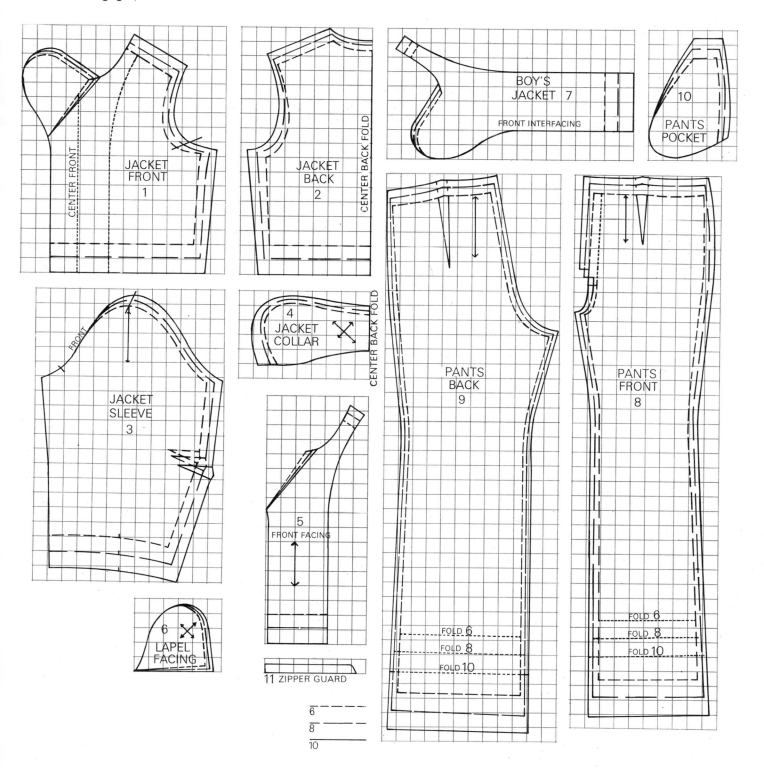

back views

1 2 3 4 5 6 7 8 9 10 11

12 13 14 15 16 17 18 19 20 21 22 23

24 25 26 27 28 29 30 31

back views

32

33

34 35

36 37

38

39

40

41

42 43

44

45 46

47

48 49

50 51 52

53

54 55

56 57

58

59

60

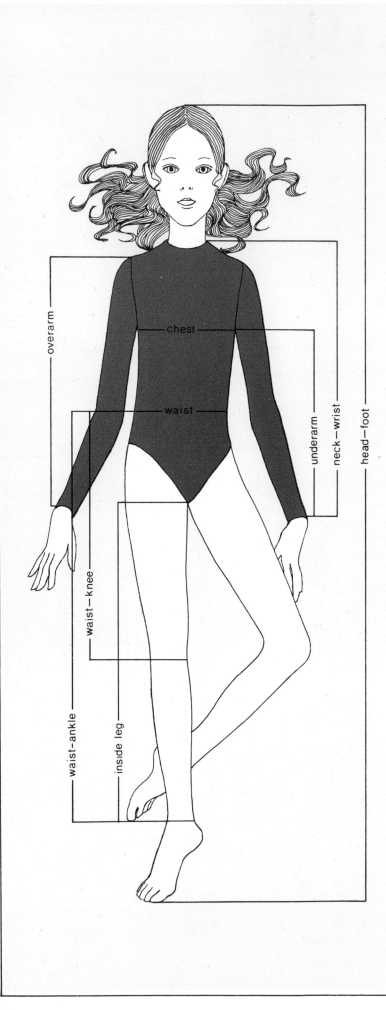

know-how

Children vary in their sizes and proportions, so check these before you begin to make your patterns. When deciding which size to make for your child, go by the chest size. Our designers had today's taller children in mind, and you can see at a glance the overall heights for which the garments were planned; adapt these lengths to suit your own child.

You will need

Sewing machine: straight stitch or with useful zigzag stitch. Needles: size 8 for dressmaking, size 9 for sewing fine fabrics and size 7 for heavier fabrics and heavier sewing, such as stitching on buttons. Pins: steel. Scissors: sharp cutting shears, small dressmaking scissors. Tailor's chalk. Tape measure. Thimble. Set square and yardstick for making patterns. Iron. Ironing board.

Before making pattern note these measurements

Chest, waist, hips, width of back, width of chest, round neck, shoulders, round arm, sleeve length, nape to waist, waist to knee. For pants, waist to crotch, inside leg to ankle. Do not measure tightly but allow tape to run closely over child's body.

table of sizes

measurements given in inches

age	length	head to foot	chest	waist	hips
1	31½—34		22	—	23½
2	36		23	23	26
3	38½		23½	23	26½
4	41		24½	23½	27½
5	43		25½	24	28½
6	45½		26	24½	30
7	48		27½	24½	31½
8	50½		28½	25	32
9	52½		29	25½	33
10	55		30	26	34
11	57½		30½	26½	34½
12	60		31½	26½	35½
13	62½		32	27	36

How to read the graphs

Patterns on graphs are all given in either two or three sizes. Follow straight line, broken line or dotted line, according to the size you need.

Each square represents one inch square.

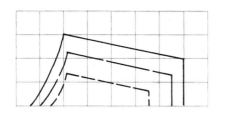

Key to sizes

Largest size ——————————
Middle size — — — — — —
Smallest size — – — – — – —

Seam allowances

These are not included on graphs. Before cutting out fabric add $\frac{3}{4}$ inch for seams, 3 inches for hems of dresses, 2 inches for hems of pants, vests, jackets, tunics, pleated skirts and ordinary seam allowance on blouse hem. On suitable designs allow $1\frac{1}{2}$ inches on lower edges of sleeves to allow for lengthening.

Ease

If you check the pattern pieces you will find they are larger than the measurements given. This is because they have 'ease' built in, so that the garment feels comfortable to wear, not skin tight. These patterns have $3\frac{1}{2}$ inches ease allowed.

Making a pattern from a graph

Use pencil, graph paper, large sheets of brown paper or newspaper (but be careful with this when using light fabrics in case newsprint makes dirty marks). Select pattern size needed and cut paper into pieces just large enough to accommodate each pattern graph, then count the squares and translate them into inches. Use set square and yardstick to draw paper up accurately into one inch squares. To copy pattern, say for bodice front, start from top left hand corner of diagram. Count squares to lower point of neck line and mark on paper. Now measure distance of upper point of neck from side and top of paper, mark and connect the two points to copy neck curve. Draw remainder of pattern to scale similarly. Copy all pattern pieces in the same way. Identify every pattern piece – back, front, skirt and so on, marking center front, center back, darts, fronts of sleeves, pockets and any other details.

Altering lengths

To alter the length of a bodice, skirt, sleeve or pants leg, find a point about one third of the way up from lower edge and draw a horizontal line across pattern. To deduct length, fold away surplus at this point. To add, cut through pattern and insert necessary amount of extra paper. Never add or deduct at hem of a flared garment as this will alter shape of flare. To alter a panty pattern, measure child through crotch from center front to center back and compare with measurement on pattern. To shorten, divide difference by four and deduct this amount equally from waist and depth of crotch, about 3 inches above crotch seam on both back and front pattern pieces. To lengthen, add difference in the same way.

Making facing pattern

Lay front pattern section on to sheet of paper, pencil round outside edges of shoulder and neck, and center front as well if pattern is not cut on a fold. Measure 2 inches for facing width and make line of pencil dots parallel to edges. Join dots to make facing outline. Repeat for back. Make armhole facing pattern in the same way. Armhole and neck facings can also be cut in one as shown.

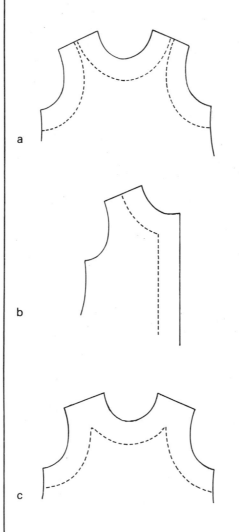

a   Neck and armhole facing
b   Combined neck and front facing
c   Combined neck and armhole facing

Cutting out

If fabric has become creased, press carefully. Leave fabric folded, wrong side out, selvages together. Place pattern pieces on fabric, following layout diagram, placing patterns on fold where indicated. Be careful with one-way fabrics where pattern or pile runs in one direction. Pattern pieces must all run in same direction. Pin pattern pieces round edges, leaving enough room between the pieces for seam allowances. Mark seam and hem allowances with sharpened tailor's chalk. Mark darts and other details with tailor's tacks.

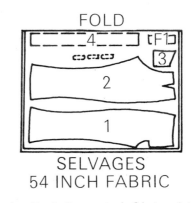

FOLD

SELVAGES
54 INCH FABRIC

(broken line indicates single fabric only)

Preparing for fitting

Children dislike standing still for long, so try to have no more than two fitting sessions. Place cut out pieces on a flat surface. Pin and baste darts. Pin and baste front to back along side and shoulder seam lines, right sides of fabric together, raw edges level, leaving center front or center back seam open so that garment is easily slipped on and off. Pin and baste skirt seams, gather skirt to correct size with running stitch if necessary. Pin and baste bodice and skirt together. Slip garment on to child. Pin together seam allowances down center opening.

Fitting points to watch

Make sure that a fitted bodice sits well and is not strained by a tight seam allowance at neck or armholes. If either is tight, carefully snip seam allowance until it lies flat. Mark new seam lines. A fitted bodice should not lie too close to the body on a little girl's dress. Give her room for energetic play. If you have to reduce any fullness at sides of a garment, pin this away evenly on both sides, but never cut away this surplus until you are absolutely sure the fit is right. If alterations are needed at shoulder line, neck and armholes must be re-marked from pattern. When you are satisfied with your adjustments, rebaste and start making up garment. Second fitting: pin and baste sleeve seams. Pin and baste sleeves into armholes, making sure they are right way round. Check sleeve and hem lengths and see that hems are straight. Adjust position of pockets or other details. If a toddler refuses to cooperate, you could measure these final details against a similar garment. Mark adjustments, unpick basting.

Common fitting problems

Dropped shoulders: Pin off required amount from outer edge of shoulder seam. Snip seam allowance around lower armhole until creases running towards underarm have disappeared, both back and front. Mark new underarm seam line if necessary.

High tummy: If dress juts out in front lift a little more fabric into side bust dart, or make a small dart if there is not one already (amount taken into dart must be added to hem line at side of dress).

Hollow back (for dress with waist seam): Lift out excess fabric into back waist seam, tapering towards side seams. A very slight amount taken out here will make a great difference to the fit.

Preparing pants for fitting

Pin and baste side seams. Pin and baste each inner leg seam. Slip left pants leg into right leg, right sides facing. Join sections along center back seam, through crotch to center front seam. Pull pants leg out.

Points to watch: See that the child can sit, bend and stoop and has enough room for easy movement. Check length. If pants are wide in waist, adjust at side seams. Mark any alterations needed. Unpick basting.

Room for growth

It is a mistake to think that a child's dress will last longer if it is made with a really deep hem. In fact, any hem over four inches deep will only add weight to the garment and can make it look shapeless. Bear in mind, too, that when a dress becomes too short for a growing child, it affects not only the hem but also the length between shoulder and underarm and this, in turn, makes the sleeves too tight. Making a garment 'on the big side' is not the answer either, because the sad result would be a new garment which is shapeless, eventually fitting only when it is worn out! Instead, make clothes that fit well right from the start, which the child can enjoy wearing and you can be proud of having made. The hem allowances we have recommended for skirts and long sleeves are adequate for lengthening if the garment is made from a suitable fabric. Be sure that stitch marks will not show after unpicking and you are able to press out the old hem line completely.

working details

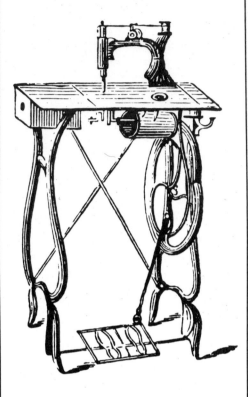

Seams and darts

Aim to run straight lines into curves gradually. Start at top of side seams, stitching just outside basting lines. Begin at base of dart and stitch just outside basting lines, tapering towards point. Secure threads at point with a knot. Where there is no dart on a back shoulder seam, back shoulder may need to be eased to front shoulder. Baste eased seam before stitching.

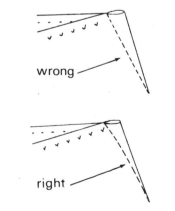

wrong

right

Pressing

Pressing means fixing a certain shape. To retain this, use a lifting and pressing movement, adjusting pressure according to fabric you are using. Woolens and linens require heavy pressure. Rayons, silks and man-made fibers need only light pressure.

If using a damp cloth for steam pressing, do not keep iron in same place until cloth is dry, but lift and press repeatedly until all steam has gone. It is a good precaution to use a dry cloth under iron, even if fabric does not require steam.

Seams: Press along stitching line then open seam with tip of iron and press. To avoid an impression on right side of fabric, slip a piece of brown paper under seam edges.

Darts: Press towards point with tip of iron. Darts on heavy fabrics should be slashed to within half inch of point and pressed open. Press shoulder and waist line darts towards center. Press underarm darts downwards. Press sleeve darts down.

Pants: Press flat when side seams are joined. When inner leg seams are joined pull each leg over sleeve board, press downwards from crotch.

Seam finishing

After seam has been pressed open oversew or use zigzag machine stitch. For armholes press seam allowances together into sleeve and press waist seams allowances upwards, then oversew seam allowances together. Do not pull oversewing stitches too tight. Snip into curves to release any tightness.

Topstitched seam

Run a row of machine stitching each side of seam, on outside of garment. Topstitch parallel to edge on collars, cuffs or pockets. For a bolder effect use buttonhole twist and a slightly larger stitch setting. If worked by hand use $\frac{1}{4}$ inch running stitches.

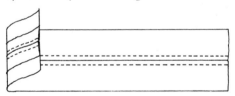

Use these two special seam techniques for neatening and strengthening a seam:

Flat fell seam

Stitch seam in normal way. Remove basting. Trim one seam allowance to $\frac{5}{8}$ and the other to $\frac{3}{16}$ inch. Press seam allowance to one side with wider seam allowance covering trimmed allowance. Turn under edge of upper seam allowance so it is level with trimmed seam. Pin and baste over trimmed seam edge. Stitch close to fold.

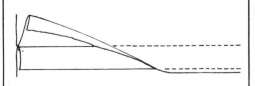

French seam

With wrong sides facing, pin and stitch seam $\frac{3}{8}$ inch from seam line in the seam allowance. Trim seam allowance and lightly press stitched seam towards front. Turn garment inside out. Working on wrong side, pin, baste and stitch along original seam line, encasing raw edges in seam.

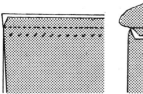

right side

Facings

Stitch back and front neck facings at shoulder seams. Press. With right sides together lay facings in position on garment with neck edges level, shoulder seams matching. Pin and baste. With facings uppermost stitch in place. Stitch armhole facings also at underarm seam then attach in same way.

On garments designed for hard wear facings can be under-stitched to seam allowances. Press both seam allowances towards facing and stitch on right side of facing, just outside seam line, through all thicknesses of allowances and facing. Turn facings to inside of garment, press in position. Lightly sew facing edges to seam allowances only.

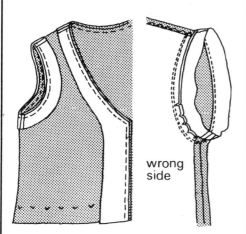

wrong side

Setting in sleeves

Pin, baste and stitch sleeve seam, then press seam open. If there is any fullness around top of sleeve cap, this must be evenly distributed. Make a line of running stitches around cap of sleeve, just outside seam line. Draw in gathering thread until sleeve fits armhole, fastening gathering thread over a pin for adjustment. Unless sleeve is puffed try to shrink away fullness by pressing over end of sleeve board, using steam on woolen fabrics but making sure that fabric does not mark. Pin sleeve into armhole, matching seams and notches. Baste and stitch in place, working with sleeve uppermost.

Putting in a zipper

Prepare opening by basting seams together along seam line. Press open carefully. Remove basting. Open zipper to bottom and lay it in opening so that seam edges just cover zipper teeth on both sides. Baste zipper into position. To make sure that seams lie perfectly flat, close zipper before you machine it in. Using a zipper foot on the machine start stitching about $\frac{3}{8}$ inch from seam edge on one side, stitch down until level with zipper end. Turn work and stitch towards seam. Pivot work on needle and return on other side in same way. Remove basting. Press gently wrong side up; nylon zippers need only the lightest touch.

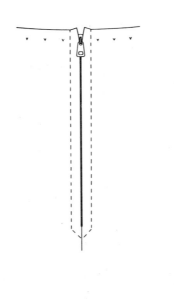

Making the pants

Stitch waist darts, if any. Stitch side seams (for boy's pants with side seam pockets see below). Press. Stitch inner leg seams, stretching upper part of back slightly to match front. Now slip the left pants leg into right, right sides facing. Pin and baste along center back seam through to center front seam (as far as zipper opening if there is one). To withstand strain on crotch seam stitch with a No. 40 mercerized cotton thread or a pure silk thread. Use shallowest zigzag stitch on machine, stretching seam a little as you stitch (otherwise use a straight stitch). Press seam open. Do not snip seam allowances at curve. Carefully press with point of iron on seam line only. Stitch along seam line again.

Boy's pants pockets: With right sides together, place pocket sections to pants fronts and backs as shown, with top edge of pocket in line with waist edge of pants. Stitch pocket to pants down side seams. Press seam allowances towards pocket. Pin and baste side seam of pants. Stich from top curved edge of pocket in one continuous seam to lower edge of pants.

Starting at waist edge stich pants front and back together for $1\frac{3}{4}$ inch at inner edge of pocket. Clip into back pants seam allowance at base of pocket. Press pocket towards front and baste top edge to waist edge of pants front.

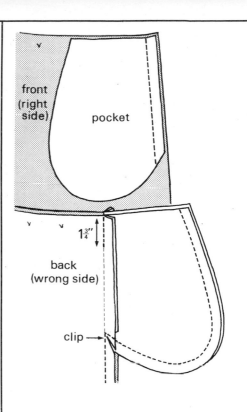

front (right side)

pocket

$1\frac{3}{4}''$

back (wrong side)

clip

Zipper guard in boy's pants: Press fly extension on both sides to inside along center front. Trim away extension on right side, leaving normal seam allowance. Stitch two sections of guard together around curved edge, right sides together. Turn right side out and press. Baste zipper in place behind opening as explained but with right side just clearing teeth. Place guard behind right hand side of zipper and stitch close to fold through all thicknesses. Stitch left hand side of zipper in place half an inch from center front fold, curving in towards base as shown.

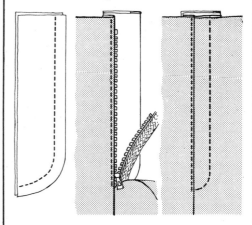

Making a collar
Collar without facings

With right sides facing and raw edges level, pin collar and under-collar together. Baste and stitch round outer edges, leaving neck edge open. Remove basting, trim seam allowance across corners and along seam edges. Turn to right side. Baste along stitched edges so that both pieces lie flat. Press lightly. Place collar to neck edge, underside to garment, baste and stitch under collar only. Press collar seam allowances upwards, turn under remaining edge and slip stitch over previous stitching line.

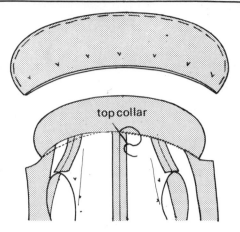

top collar

Collar with front facing

Prepare collar as above. Place collar to neck edge, under side to right of garment. Baste along neck edge through all layers. Baste bias strip over collar turnings, but only as far as shoulder seams. Fold front facings over collar and stitch along neck edge. Trim seams and turn to right side. Press and slip stitch bias strip.

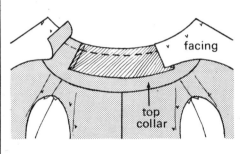

facing

top collar

Making a waist band

Fold band in half lengthways, right sides facing. Stitch narrow ends. Turn to right side. Place one long edge of band to waist seam, right sides facing, and with band extending at one end for wrap. Stitch. Trim and press seam into band. Turn in seam allowance of remaining raw edge and slip stitch to inside along seam line.

Bound buttonhole

1. Measure out buttonhole position and mark (figure 1).
2. For each buttonhole cut a strip of fabric on the cross, 2 inches wide and $1\frac{1}{2}$ inches longer than buttonhole length. Working on outside of garment lay strip centrally over buttonhole position, right sides of fabric facing (figure 2).
3. Working on wrong side of fabric and using a small stitch setting, stitch outline of buttonhole, shaping it into a perfect rectangle (figure 3) running last stitches over first to secure.
4. Using sharp pointed scissors, cut into stitched area, taking care not to cut stitches at corners (figure 4).
5. Pull binding to inside (figure 5). Press seam allowances away from opening.
6. Turn work to outside and gently roll folded edges of binding so that they meet along center of buttonhole with equal width

to each side (figure 6). Baste along opening.
7. Turn work to inside and gently pull horizontal edges of binding fabric to make rolls continue evenly beyond opening of buttonhole. Catch them together (figure 7). Press.
8. Turn garment facing over buttonholes. Baste front edge of facing into position. Feel buttonhole through facing fabric and make a cut through facing to length of buttonhole opening. Turn in edges of cut and hem to buttonhole (figure 8).
Make a small bar across each end as shown to strengthen buttonhole.

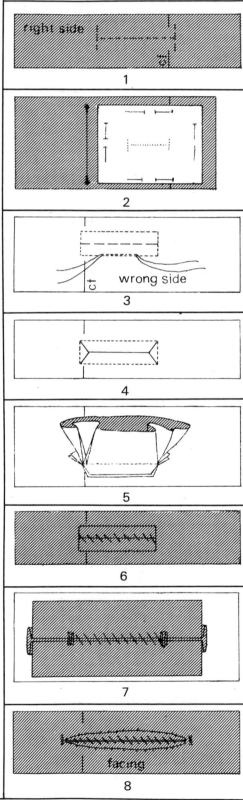

right side

1

2

wrong side

3

4

5

6

7

facing

8

Hand-worked buttonhole.

1. Mark length of buttonhole, for flat buttons diameter of button plus $\frac{1}{8}$ inch. For thick buttons add $1\frac{1}{2}$ times thickness of button.
2. Using sharp scissors, cut along button hole length. Oversew cut edges.
3. Starting with length of thread long enough to complete buttonhole, work buttonhole stitches from left to right along length of buttonhole. Do not pull loops too tight or edge will roll. If the stitches are worked too close together, the edge will cockle. Form a fan of stitches round the end of the buttonhole, keeping center stitch in line with slit. Continue along top edge of buttonhole. Make small bar across both rows of stitches at end.

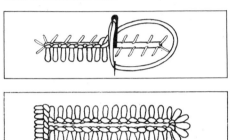

Hand-worked button loops

Use buttonhole twist. Form the loop with three strands of twist, secured with back stitches. With the same thread work blanket stitches firmly along the loop.

Interfacing

Interfacing is recommended for more tailored styles and a crisp look. Cut to shape of front neck facing, collar, cuffs as suggested.

Front: Baste in place to wrong side of front of garment, with front edge to fold line or front seam line. Catch stitch lightly down front edge. Stitch facing as normal.

Collar: Baste interfacing to wrong side of one layer of collar and use as top collar.

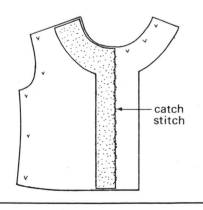

catch stitch

Sleeve with a cuff

There are two methods used in this book for making an opening at lower edge of the sleeve.

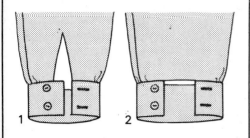

1. Slashed opening: Make a facing for opening with piece of self fabric $2\frac{1}{2}$ inches by 4 inches (for a 3 inch long opening). Neaten one end and the two long edges. Place facing to sleeve centrally along opening, right sides together, and stitch from markings at lower edge tapering to a point 3 inches in. Slash carefully to point without cutting stitching. Turn right side out and press.

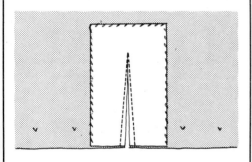

2a. Lapped opening (used on fine fabrics): Measure out the width of the opening for $\frac{3}{4}$ inch to each side of the opening mark. Trim the seam allowance along the length of the opening to $\frac{1}{2}$ inch and extend the trimming to $\frac{1}{4}$ inch beyond the marked out opening at each end (figure 1). Starting at the center of the $1\frac{1}{2}$ inch opening, roll the seam allowance under for $\frac{1}{4}$ inch and turn it under again by the same amount. Let it taper out into the raw edges just beyond the mark on each side. Hand sew the small hem firmly. When stitching on the cuff make sure that each end of the roll is firmly anchored in the stitches (figure 2).

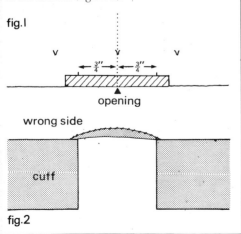

2b. Lapped opening (for heavy fabrics which do not fray): Measure out the length of opening for $\frac{3}{4}$ inch to each side of the opening mark. Run a row of small machine stitches across the opening seam line and $\frac{1}{4}$ inch beyond each side, to reinforce. Clip through seam allowance at either side (figure 3). Turn middle section to inside and herringbone in place.

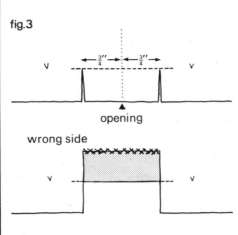

Making cuffs

Once opening has been neatened stitch sleeve seam. Press. Gather lower edge of sleeve with two rows of long machine stitches. Baste interfacing to wrong side of one half of each cuff and catch stitch along fold line. The interfaced section will go to the top of the cuff. (For cuffs with two pieces interface a complete section. Place one interfaced section to one plain section, right sides together, and stitch together along one long edge). Baste interfaced layer of cuff to gathered edge of sleeve adjusting gathers to fit and allowing 1 inch wrap on the back edge of the slashed opening. Stitch. Fold cuff lengthways, right sides together, and stitch across ends and along wrap if applicable. Layer seam allowances. Turn right side out and press seam allowances into cuff. Turn in remaining edge of cuff and slip stitch in place over seam line.

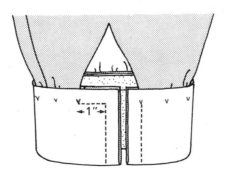

Making a hem

Always pin at right angles to hem. Make sure that hem depth is even all round. Working with hem lying flat on table, baste hem about $\frac{1}{2}$ inch from lower edge. Press from wrong side, with hem lying flat on ironing board.

Invisibly hemming a flared skirt

Prepare as above. Then use small running stitch to gather in fullness along raw edge and draw it up to fit skirt, making sure that fullness is evenly distributed. Oversew raw edge by hand. Baste about $\frac{3}{4}$ inch from upper edge. Taking depth of hem in your hand, without creasing it, turn over $\frac{1}{4}$ inch of upper edge. Sew invisibly behind hem as shown, taking up very little thread from the skirt and a good deep thread from the hem.

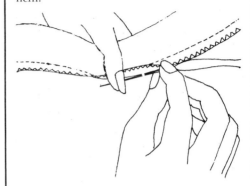

Invisible herringbone

Same technique as invisible hemming but with herringbone stitch, catching fabric from garment and hem. This method is good for heavier fabrics.

Straight hem

Turn raw edge under $\frac{1}{2}$ inch, slip stitch to garment. When hemming long sleeves, keep stitches close together to prevent child's fingers catching. Pants hems should be no more than 2 inches deep.

Making up and inserting a jacket lining

Cut out lining using 36 inch layout but omitting facings. If center back is to a fold allow an extra inch for pleat (for ease of movement). Stitch side, shoulder and sleeve seams. Press. Press in one inch pleat in center back and secure with cross stitches for three inches from neck edge.

Pin lining to jacket, wrong sides facing, matching seam lines. Trim away one inch from front and neck edges, turn in $\frac{1}{2}$ inch and slip stitch in place over facings. Baste around armhole. Slip sleeve lining into sleeve, wrong sides facing. Turn in seam allowance at top of sleeve and fell in place over jacket lining. Turn up hem of jacket and sleeve lining and slip stitch in place $\frac{1}{2}$ inch above fabric hem.

Making pleats

Before cutting garment be sure fabric is perfectly square on the grain. Do this by drawing out a thread and cutting along drawn thread line. Make hem before pleating. A 2 inch hem is sufficient as it is difficult to lengthen a pleated garment. Press hem carefully. Mark pleats with fabric right side up, pleat in direction indicated, marking each pleat line with a line of pins. Fold each pleat, bringing the fold over to fall on pleat depth line. Baste down securely. Press carefully. Secure upper edge of pleating with row of machine stitching just above waist seam.

Shirring

Wind shirring yarn on to bobbin, lengthen stitch and loosen top tension (experiment with shirring yarn and spare fabric). Mark fabric with basting lines the distance apart required by design. Work on right side, leaving long threads at ends of rows which can be drawn up to take away more fullness if necessary. Fasten off by hand with several small back stitches.

Bias binding

1. Commercial bias binding has two creases already pressed in. It should be opened out and placed to the edge to be bound with the first crease along the seam line. Stitch, trim seam, press. Turn binding to inside along seam line and slip stitch in place (figures 1 and 2).

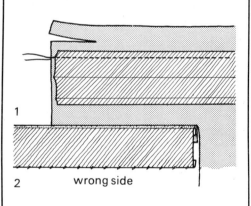

2. Where binding is intended to show no seam allowance is necessary on edge to be bound. Place binding to fabric, right sides together, raw edges level, and stitch along first crease line of binding. Turn second crease line of binding to inside and slip stitch to seam line (figures 3 and 4).

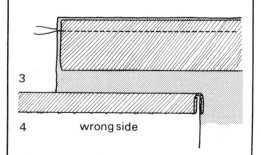

Self binding: This is made from strips of the garment fabric cut on the bias. Both above methods of application are suitable for self bias binding except, of course, you do not have creases to guide you.

Soft belt with buckle

Fold fabric lengthways, right sides facing. Stitch belt, leaving ends open and opening about 3 inches long half way along stitching line. Press seam open, it must lie flat at center, on inside of belt. Stitch end of belt, shaping into point if required. Trim seam allowances. Turn belt to right side by pushing ends through opening over blunt end of knitting needle. Fold in edges of opening and slip stitch. Attach buckle, folding left end of belt over bar. Turn raw edge under and stitch firmly.

Tie belt: Make as above but stitch both narrow ends before turning.

Making up panties

Stitch side seams with a French seam. To make casing for elastic at waist edge, turn under raw edge $\frac{1}{4}$ inch, then the remainder of seam allowance. Stitch in place, leaving opening to insert elastic. Also stitch upper edge to stop it rolling over. Insert elastic. Make casings for elastic on legs with bias strip of fabric or bias binding.

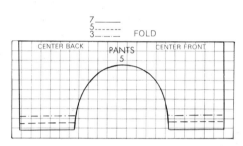

Working with jersey

Marking pattern detail: Use a soft thread such as a No. 50 basting cotton. Sharp thread can cut jersey stitches.

Stitching: Reduce pressure on presser foot of machine as jersey tends to spread. Use finest needle size and pure silk thread. Engage shallowest zigzag stitch and stitch length setting of 12 to 14 stitches per inch. Gently stretch seams when stitching to give maximum elasticity. Seams which have to bear strain should be stitched over twice.

Seam finishes: Unnecessary.

Darts: Slash along center and press open.

Making hem: Use invisible herringbone stitch for extra strength and 'give'.

Working with velvet

Cutting out: Decide which way you want pile to run. For a rich effect the pile should go upwards. However, if the garment is to be worn a lot, dirt will get less ingrained if the pile runs downwards.

Keep direction of pile consistent. If working on a folded layout, keep pile facing outwards.

Marking pattern detail: Use fine soft thread such as pure silk. Be sparing with tailor's tacks, working outside stitching line.

Stitching: Pressure of upper presser foot on machine must be reduced, unless machine is self adjusting. Test by placing two scraps of velvet face to face. Stitch with pure silk. If seam begins to wring, loosen pressure. Try again until seam remains flat. Adjust stitch tension if you have difficulty: a tightly set stitch tension will cause seams to pucker. If necessary a second row of basting just outside seam line will give seam more support.

Seam finishes: Hand sew.

Zippers: Use strong dress zipper. Hand sew.

Making hem: Velvet dresses cannot be let down. Reduce hem allowance to $1\frac{1}{2}$ inches, ease in fullness around top edge of hem allowance, neaten and hand sew with invisible hemming.

Pressing: Use a needleboard if possible. Fabric is pressed with pile down on needleboard. Otherwise, draw seams over iron standing on its end and covered with damp cloth. Open seam allowance and draw seam section by section over iron, pat velvet gently with soft brush.

Corduroy and needlecord

Cutting: Remember to keep direction of pile consistent as with velvet. It is easier to mark fabric on wrong side.

Pressing: Work on wrong side, using as little pressure as possible.

Working with toweling

Be sure to wash fabric before you begin to make it up as toweling shrinks.

Cutting out: Do not use too many pins as pinning through thick fabric could reduce size of pattern.

Seams: Normal on single toweling, flat fell seams, $\frac{1}{2}$ to $\frac{3}{4}$ inch wide, for double-sided toweling.

Pressing: If loops become slightly flattened, brush up with flat of your hand while still warm to make them rise again.

Zippers: Hand sew.

Fur fabric

Cutting out: Fur fabric has a woven or knitted backing. In either case lay the fabric pile side down, and cut one layer at a time, keeping pattern pieces on straight grain of backing. Mark round pattern pieces with tailor's chalk and cut backing with sharp blade, taking care not to cut the pile.

Stitching: Stitch with strong needle and a thread with elasticity such as a pure silk or synthetic thread. Experiment on scraps for stitch tension. Separate hairs of pile before stitching. When stitched use a pin to pull out pile along seam line and trim away pile on seam allowances. Press with cool iron.

After care: Fur fabrics are made from a variety of man-made or natural fibers. Be sure to ask about after care when buying and carefully follow manufacturers instructions. Experiment on scraps for pressing.

Working with quilted fabric

Cutting out: Fold fabric right side out.

Marking pattern detail: For darts and other details, make single tailor's tacks through slits in pattern. For seam lines use colored chalk. First pin pattern pieces to fabric along seam lines, catching both layers in the pins. Open seam allowance to get to wrong side of fabric, make chalk mark over each pin where you can see or feel it.

Basting: Avoid wherever possible as stitches are difficult to remove, basting must be at least ¼ inch away from seam line. Leave pins in seam line to serve as guide, removing each just before needle reaches it.

Stitching: Usual sewing thread and slightly larger stitch setting. Ease pressure on presser foot or work will stick under needle.

Seam finishes: Bind seams and all raw edges with bias binding to stop fraying.

Making hem: Reduce hem allowance to 2 inches, deep hems on quilted garments tend to need frequent repairs. Finish with herringbone stitch.

Pressing: Treat as man-made fiber but do not use steam or damp cloth. This would flatten quilting.

Buttonholes: Hand-sewn, first machine stitching around outline of buttonhole to prevent layers of fabric moving. When buying quilted fabric, check that both fabric and wadding are washable.

Working with reversible fabric

Either or both sides of the material can be used as the top fabric. When working with a tweed/plain cloth it is easier to work the plain side, so treat this as the inside of the garment even when making it reversible. The two parts of a reversible fabric can be gently separated.

Garment edges: Separate layers to allow ⅜ inch to be turned in, then overcast folded edges together.

Hems: Turn up plain cloth on to tweed. Trim away tweed ⅜ inch, turn under plain side and slip stitch.

Pockets: Separate layers, turn in seam allowances and slip stitch together.

Buttonholes: Hand made.

Binding with braid

Prepare edge of garment by basting facings to inside, wrong sides facing, raw edges level. Stitch ⅛ inch inside seam line. Trim off seam allowance. Side of braid which will be uppermost should be stitched on first. Pin braid ⅜ inch from raw edge, leaving ½ inch extending to neaten later. Stitch braid into place, mitering corners. Turn braid over raw edge and cover stitching line on underside with edge of braid. Hand-sew edge of braid to garment with felling stitches.

motif library

Trace these motifs onto some of the garments in this book for a final decorative effect